POEM

BITTEN

BY A

MAN

NIGHTBOAT

NEW YORK BOOKS

POEM BITTEN BY A MAN

BRIAN TEARE

ISBN: 978-1-643-62210-1

Cover Design and Typesetting by Kit Schluter
Typeset in Cormorant Garamond and Glaser Stencil

Cataloging-in-Publication Data Is Available
from the Library of Congress

Nightboat Books
New York
www.nightboat.org

for my friends & my caregivers

& the beloved elders we've lost –

with gratitude for you all

companions of the open

I have composed a careful & on one level truly meant narrative
& on another level the Narrative of a Scissor

—SUSAN HOWE

From now on the subject says: "Hello object!" "I destroyed you."
"I love you."

—D. W. WINNICOTT

/ \

Strange indeed that illness has not taken its place with love &
battle & jealousy among the prime themes of literature.

—VIRGINIA WOOLF

It is enough to have brought poetry & painting into relation as
sources of our present conception of reality.

—WALLACE STEVENS

\ /

which portion of reality is most fragile
                              mine
        or the one in which others see me?

—GLORIA GERVITZ
TR. MARK SCHAFER

shielding my face with a scrap of red paper,
which means *I'm choosing to answer*
with this abstract shape.

—CHIYUMA ELLIOTT

The poem begins when all the tools I use to write it break / I don't know why. I open the notebook: wide graphite lines, narrow rule, useless. Then I what. Pick them up & move them about. An imagined unit, a transformation, possibility in gray! San Francisco winter, my head against the window. Thin, rinsed light of another doctor's appointment. *Coller*, "to paste," downplays the violence of the cut that comes first – disgust

                                                to give up   to get rid of

            the language value of anything at all

                                or to do the work

to doubt that the work needs doing

                                                before it exists on paper
it exists in the mind not thinking form, space, line, contour. Writing makes an *I* out of this situation: waiting room, pain scale, color field, patient history, pale tile of the clinic bathroom. Then I what. Take a number. Why. Nausea, collage, headache, these works on paper. A way to begin. To pursue meaning through its displacement. To understand change, remarkable or hidden. To go on – still thinking about painting.

Being ill in my thirties is like certain paintings from the 60s, Agnes Martin saying *yes* to the grid & *no* to pretty much everything else. Rational & fetishistic, disciplined & obsessive, her tape & ruler & graphite lines floating on canvas. Like any sign, a symptom becomes abstract through repetition until illness too seems double-voiced, a materiality that says *yes* to what, that says *no* to what, is what I ask, negotiating

define *object*   define *event*

move the "inside" of the picture

between invisible & visible

the ineffable & the clinic

what's considered to be the "material"

flower   fruit   phallus   book & vase

what principles obeyed, what principles refused, embodied by what materials & processes, the morning I vomit between parked cars & stand up, fog rolling off Twin Peaks

not a drawing   not a structure

not a speech   not a construction

with a stained collar I go to the doctor & now here is Jasper Johns, who writes in his sketchbook, "It is what it does. What can you do with it?"

FLAG, 1954-55 (1)

Encaustic, oil & collage on fabric mounted on wood (3 panels)
41 ¼ x 60 ¾ inches

to read a painting   to read a page   is to live overlapping moments   flattened on a plane

a site of love & aggression   every object of study   a fantasy object   that survives

the inevitable   reader who says hello   dear other   i destroyed you   i love you

a technique   of individuation   & an inescapable condition   of cultural production

to paint a flag   means design's taken care of   johns says in 1959   it gives me room

to work on other levels   which other levels   does he mean ?   critics ask for decades

the commonplace as a painting   its affect flat as a slap   it's the military application

of visual techniques   for focusing desire   or aggression   an affront to certain histories

of art   graphic design   nationhood   & aren't there *other*   other levels ?   i ask the flag

as i pull back   the bedsheet beneath   layers of newspaper   & tinted wax   & lie down

not *really* collage   a critic says   not *really* encaustic   the dream of a former soldier

with a new boyfriend   & an estranged alcoholic father   dead the day before his first show

the flag's a fantasy   of love & destruction   emblem of everything   conflicted inside him

the flag's an affect   wide as migraine   debilitating & interesting   to lie down inside

The day I move in with R my father dies into a more permanent estrangement than alcohol. In bed I can't shake the sensation of movement – our new blue bedroom like the prow of a ship headed into the Pacific, the sky now like an egg with the top lopped off, gelid ruddy sun ringed in white. In his sketchbook Johns believes painting to be a language. *Ut pictura poesis*, sort of. In the notebook I copy

        Foreground
        Background

                Figure as a space (or hole?)
                in the _____ (landscape?)

the way a painting hangs
outside its maker, never-ending, the only thing in the world both continuous & still. The problem is how to make language more, a dimension that holds & meets multiple demands: love, work, death, art. & gut trouble, joint pain, headaches that last for days. I write it all down

            Competition as definition
            of one kind of focus

            Competition (?) for different
            kinds of focus

What prize? What price?

        We can't afford to fly to the funeral. My father's body goes into the Alabama ground. Like burying a compass – it's not much use there. "When the rose is destroyed, we grieve" writes Agnes, "but really beauty is unattached & a clear mind sees it." Each night bedded down with R in sleep's bluest boat I think I hear a foghorn guide us through the Golden Gate to open ocean.

In the archives of abstraction I hold pages of Agnes' handwriting –
on lined paper, school-girl cursive round & very neat. I love artist's
writings the way I love handwriting, its adjacency to drawing.
Sincere open loops like her ruddy cheeks, her manuscript has the
look of dictation, it bears so few corrections. Johns in his
sketchbooks truly tries things out, betraying proximity to his own
embodied life where events occur without permission. Though
finished artworks try to hide it, "finish" is often predicated upon
denying the interdependence of the object & the artist's body, how
easily numbers slip into alphabets & into body parts & colors. For a
long time I lie in pain on the doctor's examination table's awkward
paper, afraid to rip it / to move my body / to move my mouth /
to move the words / to leave a trace

                                        shifting the object   drives form

                                        in a certain way   2 systems

                                        figure   ground   irregular

The way painters summon a color through touch, a feeling gathers in my gut, continuous gesture a little closer to orange, each thought not a long brushstroke but rough, interrupted, moving toward fragment, notation, parataxis. A feeling of being cold from *inside* my body. Thoraco-lumbar core ache

~~areas of red, y, blue ?~~

fill (?) the
space loosely.

I want a theory of embodied life that is also a poetics, a technique for writing without "violation of the central self." What's that. What I too often leave out: three part-time jobs, two side hustles, unpredictable pay. "You can't *make* life or art," R says, "You have to work in the gap between." Then I what. Begin with the possibilities of the materials & let them do what they can do

⟶ Space everywhere

(objects, no objects)

MOVEMENT

to accommodate
the actual / Depositing $185 from a freelance gig I'm still overdrawn. -$2.58 for the week's groceries. To finish the job I'd left everything else unfinished ⟶ to be exact, I'd left everything *in writing* unfinished. Debt again settles in my body next to illness. Chronic shift in my central self. Low-income art. Symptomatic art. Everything connected below the surface.

Heartbeat of paper

a somatic language. "Every material has
several possibilities," Ruth Asawa writes in her college notebook,
"Let's find out." Listening to these pages, I move my body from
paper to paper to paper to paper continuous as the single strand of
wire she loops into biomorphic sculpture, gorgeous invagination.
"I always begin on the inside

                    / she knits
                         gold

                                             the outside surface
                                             inside the next

in this photo the tips
of several fingers bandaged as she loops the wire to itself, abstracting
the material. *Abstractus*, both "incorporeal" & "isolated, secluded."
But I like abstraction best when I've seen the hands that made it.
I like the photo more knowing her friend Imogen Cunningham
trades three years of photographs for house repairs done by Asawa's
architect husband. Even her mentor Josef Albers, Bauhaus formalist,
teaches

                                   never to see anything
                                   in isolation

                                   define space
                                   define an object

                                   by defining the space
                                   around it

ideas
that aren't solved don't have shapes yet like the white space around
these lines. During the war, the State seizes her family's Southern
California farm & interns them all in Rohwer, Arkansas. At Black
Mountain, she falls in love with a white man from Georgia. In
San Francisco, years ago not far from here, Cunningham brings
homemade Satsuma jam to her door, first gift of a friendship from
which more forms flow.

for Kathleen Fraser

When rain blows in from the Pacific, the windows rattle in their frames. At my desk I listen to the building touch itself & tremble. One small wall heater in the flat's front room, we wear sweaters to bed. I've never lived with a lover before. I haven't loved anyone so helplessly since I was an infant, which means I can't see R clearly at all. I just hand myself over to him the way a nurse gives a swaddled newborn to its mother. After visiting us, Kathleen warns I'll have to fight for my writing; she says she can tell he won't make space

> dear other   i address him
>
> in sentences   each word
>
> a precedent for what new
>
> order   forward movement

                                        to live a creative life
/ Money makes it hard from the start. Sometimes Kathleen takes me to lunch in a glamorous swoop of laughter, a tiny black convertible in which I barely fit. Grand in a messy head scarf & chunky jewelry, she makes me think poetry might be possible in this city. But she *has* money, sends me home with bread & leftovers, a gift I share with R on the couch in front of a space heater the way I want to share what I learn from her poems, the powerful field of her reality. But I don't yet know

> how to begin   to talk to him
>
> to bring into words   fragments
> i conspire with him   to hide
>
> it is part of my commitment
> to him & myself   it is my politics
>
>   & my love

I break language at an angle

                              to ordinary life, a little awkward, the
way one leg of this thrift store chair is shorter than the others. The
words rock as I write. My father a book that has slipped into the
grass, I search for it everywhere: Agnes with her hand-drawn grids,
the appropriated commonplaces of early Johns. What I'm looking
for isn't paternal, it's tactically adjectival, *queer* like when her grid's
edges are messy, like when his canvas incorporates domestic objects

                              the image arrives

                         what does it displace
                         what does it bring

this summer of the word *quotidian*
its index of particulars, poetic or tragic murmurings, all the daily
drama of the body, oil & charcoal on canvas with objects. Of illness
there still remains little record in the literature: appearing to us as
lost to us, its abstract states persist as pain I can point to but no
one can see. I wish it were paint / I say it feels like a wire hanger's
twisted neck, an arrangement in a system to pointing. What else to
say about what's familiar & why what seems so at first turns out to
be

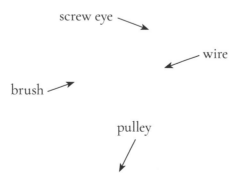

How to say what can't be seen?

Painting knows it's not the event
that matters most but the structure of feeling it leaves behind.
Agnes is a disciplinarian to disappoint, a narrow path to happiness.
My attachment a mixture of fact & fantasy, to argue with her ideas
gives shape to an agency I feel I don't have

from an object of
contemplation, an object wrapped up in identification. I try to
make her & Johns as independent of myself as I can. This is why
autobiography's so impossible. I too am a figure in a book, unreal
to myself. An object hardly inhabited

illness, always arguing
with someone besides myself. Johns for instance. When I look at
his flags

my body like a painting made with a desire to put
things into it / my body like a painting I can stand in front of &
think *I would put this into it* / the idea that things exist & you can put
them into a space / then you can have the idea

sort of sexual
& sort of formal, the way I stand naked in front of R & think

When I look at grids Agnes made in the 60s, someone has just woken up, made her bed & left the room: residual warmth travels up through intimate order. Its stringent fragrance lingers, pine resin & eucalyptus. A certain kind of person would want to turn back the blanket & seek the last of their lover's heat held in the sheet beneath. I too covet a surface sensitive to impression the way R's cheek above his beardline feels like paper made with cotton. I didn't mean to write that – I meant to touch it

                                        Color A
                                        Over
                                        Color B

            We got that
            a long time ago.
            There it is

when I look
at drawings Johns made in the early 60s. Someone has also just left the room. But he has left behind a skin, oil sprayed with powdered graphite, fixed with what? He has several likenesses, like stars & years, like numerals & this spot on the bed, invisible until I turn on the light. Wet to the touch, scent of salt & blossoming pear, white on white. The way *intimate* descends from *intus*, atmosphere of supreme lucidity, I write this from within within.

                                        fixture of pollen & semen

& Agnes in her work even less a friend of embodied life than Johns, who for a time in the 60s presses his body against paper the way David Hammons does in Los Angeles. In photos documenting his process, Hammons torques his oiled upper body onto paper laid out on his studio floor. In prints like *Black First, American Second* he wraps the resulting bodies in American flags, a strong contrast to Johns' tonally ambiguous *white* flag. While Johns' *Skin* series suggests a ready pathos critics like to read in light of his breakup with R, I like to see Johns' splayed body mark his open secret's visible limits. I like especially a photo of him mashing his greased white smooth cheek against paper pinned to his studio wall, awkward posture he avoids in earlier work. I write this in bed where the ground of writing is always the way the materiality of language meets the materiality of my body: the notebook's support records the slippage that occurs when writing's twice, constrained by chronic pain. "The mind makes marks," Johns writes, "language, measurements." & the artist's body does too, the way I always tear the examination table's thin paper, a sound that reminds me of bouncing the rent check

ideas which have been freed

from events which brought them

into being   not the object

in which different systems exist

At night the bedroom door rattles in its jamb. A storm's coming;
its dropping pressure pulses in my ears until I hear my heart beat
there. I wake & think

                my mother. I hear the horn of a tornado
warning – on the horizon a funnel turns against sallow sky.

                                        R also
has fallen in love with someone he can't see clearly. We become
more real to each other as we cuddle on the couch & watch films
that reveal our deeper preoccupations. I weep during Barbara
Loden's *Wanda* in a way I don't when my father dies. "Your
problem is you feel closer to art than people." Not closer to – safer
with

      in the basement I worry the tornado will come straight over
& it does. I can't remember the noise, the chaos – just eerie quiet
after it passes, then stuck in the dark

                            my life above ground gone

                            passive   wandering around

                            not having any direction

                            I spend years of my life that way

                            not aware of the situation I'm in

I dream this after we watch *Wanda*.
Into loving R I bring all the places I've never been safe, how the
river valley I'm from chutes tornados through town, how there's
this extreme long shot of Wanda picking her way across a coal field
that feels like my rural childhood, my mother's capacity to reduce
my life to nothing. Always I see my far queer body through her
estranging eye as through a keyhole in a locked door.

Little shrine or altar –

                              box of papers, worship's structure –

the notebook bound to household gods. There's some ceremony
in opening it, adjacency to the sacred. Ephemeral, local divinities
preside inside, a charged atmosphere my hand enacts

                                                        at home here

                                                no single thought
                                                my thought

some are found, some given, others bribed.
Whether accident, intention, or opportunity, all gods require
offerings, their acute narcissism a place in which I can hide – until
my failures accumulate weight

                              on the wrong side of favor

                                              autobiography –
one thing after another, seasons, weather, friends, awareness of
existence & mortality. Agnes the god of empty forms, of
transcendence, a personable classical impersonality. Johns the
god of the given world, of assemblage, an austere romantic
modernism. R the trickier intimacy, the failure of representation.
Other gods come & go, trailing ions that elicit thought, neural
cascades. Chronic aesthete

                                        I *do* love what I've found

                the possibility

                                        the privilege of being here, suffering
the mortal together.

Painting's endless present tense.

My experience of life is that it's very fragmented. I love it like I love deictic words, whose meaning depends on & points to their context.

In one place, certain kinds of things occur, a whole canvas of gestures that say *this & this & this here now now now,* the painter deciding yes & no with this stencil & this brush & *in another place, a different kind of thing occurs.*

Symptoms are deictic too, pointing to a context of which they are the only signs, no paint or wooden ball or ruler on a board. *I would like my work to have some vivid indication of those differences.*

Illness an object curiously caught up in its own activity, entities splitting into hand, feather, string, sponge, rag, comb. In what ways can I use the objects illness makes of me?

A drawing made behind my back. Chicken wire as a canvas. An invisible drawing, made in air. A stolen painting.

find <u>one</u> way to describe the event & the objects

I choose making with a lack of time, money, health & health insurance – lacks that mark making indelibly.

                                        is this best shown
by "pointing" to it or by "hiding" it

                                I think of the early Johns, for
whom a painting is both event & object. Q: What kind of event? A: the nature of the object produced during such a period. Sick in bed / then I what. Cut up the archives of abstraction & my notebooks

                                the elements should neither fit
nor not fit together

                a clear object   an unclear object

what kind of object? It <u>IS</u> what it <u>DOES</u>. Collage puts pressure against lived constraints until the image begins to acquire its own history, something like the surplus of an action. These assemblages do not resemble precarious employment, low income, illness, or medical debt – & they propose new ways to experience them

        the application of the eye   the business of the eye

the event provides the occasion for the object, whose nature is produced by the event. Almost tautological. Not freedom, but more room to move.

Writing & revising, cutting & pasting, typesetting & proofing: the printed poem resists the inscription of the physical acts of its making. Unless you ask where, in relation to object & event, is the poet's own body

        buttock   foot   hand   sock

the typesetter's body

                to pick up these things & move them about

within the body politic. The way it moves about in us, each color a visible action. Each line refers to historical forces experienced as personal event, the artist assuming responsibility for being, however accidentally, alive here & now.

                    "Beware of the body & the mind," Johns cautions, "Avoid a polar situation." What kind of body & what kind of mind in what kind of society? Worried about medical debt, I dream

                            it is always true
that they can be shifted

       that anything be any color & be anywhere

            that any color be anywhere & anything

a handful of wet hair falls through the mail slot!

In the archives of abstraction I read the poet's notebooks. Thom Gunn, white gay man same generation as Johns, Cold War men like my father: b. 1929, 1930, 1933. I'm looking, as always, for direction, for how to do this. "I pass the romantic impulse through the classical scrutiny," Gunn writes, "The scrutiny is both the experience & the poem's form." Johns shares this bifurcated sensibility:

> the watchman falls
> "into" the "trap" of looking
>
> the "spy" is a different
> person   ready to move
>
> aware of his entrances
> & exits   remembering

men of that era,
so self-conscious! "The spy must remember himself," Johns argues, "& his remembering," though he's designed to be overlooked, unlike the watchman, conspicuous. Years ago when I see Gunn read at an uptight upscale venue, he wears tight jeans & leather chaps & flags left red. "My impulse to write poetry so closely connected—so much a part of—my sexual impulse," he writes, "the same kind of concentrated excitement that lights up everything in a limited area

> (as a flashlite lights up
> everything in the circle
>
> it makes
>
> / not spying
>
> just looking

"we made portraits of ourselves
when we had no idea who we were"

WHITE FLAG, 1955

Encaustic, oil & collage on fabric (3 panels)
78 ¼ x 120 ¾ inches

for Lauren Berlant

the flag's an affect   white as migraine   debilitating & interesting   to lie down inside

the surface churn of pigment & wax   & figure how i feel   beginning with structure

a layer of paper & cloth collage   over stretched sateen   sensual bedclothes of a rough fuck

paramnesia streaked with semen   the way sexuality hooks up with national fantasy   queer

& visited by crippling symptoms   in the visual field of citizenship   i've been here before

as a boy i earn a badge of merit   learning to handle the flag correctly   it takes a long time

to remember all the rules   to fold & store it properly   it's the gentlest i have seen

the white fathers who teach us   who take more care with that fabric than they do with

a sissy   afraid of their cold war masculinity   indifferent to their curriculum of flags

targets & maps   i fashion a passionate impassivity   in the locker room a lot

like jasper johns   his ready-made images   *i like about them, that they come that way*

he says   *i am very stupid, politically, actually*   he says   pretty much like a jock strap

holding state knowledge   a site of the full coming together of violence & reason

dear johns   thank you for the headache   i hate your archive   a faggot has no true flag

A heatwave in the middle of the feeling called *money*. Days in the 90s, collages built up like diary entries. The concrete holds sun to the extent that memory becomes part of the composition, the present I carry with me. Too little shade from too few trees while I wait for the bus. Shit, puke & piss a radiant stink.

> Think of the
> edge of the city &
> the traffic there

when I turn away to work R can't bear it & makes
writing his rival. To ease his enmity, I stop writing. This place
where I repair my relationship to the world, without time &
solitude I can't enter it

> to make relation bearable

> we talk
about a bolt to replace the broken latch on the study door he can't
keep himself from opening when I try to write. *Hello, love*, I say. All
the while knowing the world, of course, is unbearable. Why
bother? I don't want to choose

> Distinguishing one thing from another

> Somewhere here, there is the
> question of "seeing clearly"

> Seeing <u>what</u>?
> <u>According to what</u>?

the only real surprise
will be if I ever succeed at all.

The painted line differs from the written line.

Glyph or grammar, the difference has something to do with time, the way I open the notebook then the laptop years later, write then type, fold seconds into each syllable, minutes into each sentence, the selves of each moment cool & creased as they collapse into pleats.

It sounds like a fan but it's more phantasmal, how we joke my memoir of this time will be *Jasmine & Feces*, perennial scents of our block. All the spent years touch *here* & *here*. For a long time the flat feels like the sweetest vocative, intimate address in our bedroom blue as a naïve dreamer's idea of water.

I turn onto Albion Street & round the corner into unfinished memory, what I don't write down, the notebook months of raw canvas where color should be.

Wordless – there are no words for it. Wordless – I won't or can't bring myself to write it. Wordless – "Don't write about me," R commands.

However long it takes, wordlessness *is* work. Like a migraine I wait until biography's the right size for writing.

Horrible aura, we wake when the meth lab across the street blows up. Electrical coruscations, smoke in puffy scumbled charcoal. We close the windows. Here at last I write the line of blackened jasmine, crusted with grit the color of dogshit.

"To the detached person," writes Agnes, "the complication of the involved life is like chaos." I cut open the sentence to let it in, shadow & origin. My body resists resting its headache on the mat in supplication. Part arthritis, part ego. Then I what. Insist like the monk leading zazen, dismissing limitation, tatami cool on my forehead until I can't bear the pain. Humbled, I like to think what I write after acknowledges

The painted space / the space of painting
seems mutable

Things which were not there can appear
in it or be put into it

at the border of the ordinary

the mistake of a tragedy's protagonist

seeking suffering's end, I only add to it
/ A sleeper leaning harder into a difficult dream. "To feel removed from the work, neutral toward it," Johns says of his flags, numbers & maps, "Involved in the making, but not involved in the judging of it." Sort of like everyday life, whose surface appears impassive, the notebook holds something like chaos between its covers & can't contain it.

Is there any need to enhance
this characteristic?

Just enough self-awareness to wonder what's the best syntax for shitting myself in public. *I don't like the medium, although I'm going to do some more.*

Sticky, warm, densely scented, the self I become soiled still blocks from home, "human" & "humiliation" sharing the root "humus." *That line. You draw a line & it has a very sensitive, sort of human quality.*

"Reason rooted in the bowels of the earth," this sense of life a language "more sensual, more obscene," I mean <u>really</u> shitting literature myself.

There is the distraction of the line, which takes on the quality of a seismography, as if the body were the earth. Fumbling with the keys, I yell, fucking lock, fucking door, R trying not to laugh.

There are fantastic things happening in the black ink, & none of those things are what one had in mind. In the house of literature, I lock myself in the bathroom with a rag. I stand in the tub & strip, wash myself clean as the nib of this pen.

Both Agnes & Johns maintain certain sanctities associated with good taste. Agnes is single- though not simple-minded about it, & even the greedily heterogeneous Johns brooks little vulgarity after the infamous green penis in 1955's *Target with Plaster Casts*. I think about this when Jesse the phlebotomist taps a vein, when I piss in the plastic cup & screw on its yellow cap. Often when I look at their work, the museum's the ground & their paintings are figures

2 figures, one ground   duet

idea of neutrality   body as tube

what's irregular is the distribution of wealth, the way *vulgar*'s root is *vulgus*, "the common people." Their profitable assimilation into museums & private collections has everything to do with tacit markers of race & class. Biohazard & test subject, here my body makes *its* marks, mortal work in which I'm as implicated as the rusty splotch left in lifted gauze. A bit bruised already, I wash my hands & slip the warm cup through the little clinic window.

During the years preceding her 1967 psychotic break, Martin lives on Coenties Slip & Johns on Pearl & then Front Street, a short distance neither crosses to the other. Her biographer argues "Johns was developing a language that had much in common with Martin's." Would either agree with that? In the early 60s certain of their canvasses might have a passing resemblance, but Martin's metaphysical obsessions are informed in part by visionary experience. Johns has aesthetic obsessions informed in part by the gay male coterie of R, Cage & Cunningham, & in part by art history, Duchamp in particular. Abstraction for her means a fairly limited vocabulary, whereas for him it means

\

a rearrangement

the air must move

in as well as out

of "the painted space." Not the grid's fixity, but a dexterous restlessness, meaning's mutability & manipulability

no sadness

just disaster

I prefer code to confession

                                because I'm the worst person in this
building, worse than the junky couple downstairs who set their
bedroom on fire, worse than the girl upstairs who leaves her flat
with the pilot light out & the gas oven running, worse than the
firefighters who bang down each door while we stand on the
sidewalk, worse than housefire or asphyxiation

                                        unlovable
                                        unfuckable
                                        unreasonable

                                                illness
an unpredictable gender, my preferred pronoun a fucking
meltdown. The way Eva Hesse's late sculptures look each day I
spend with them, suspended from hooks in loops or sheets, leaning
in tubes or lying flat, some a sag or collapse of discarded skin, some
flung resinous strings, mucus-colored & muscular – all of them
uncannily bodily, possessed of such *posture* in relation to space
around them

                thinking working. doing.
                ill should not matter to

                                        description
                                        A thing
                                        the thing
                                        is made

                                        I leave the museum
with her late shapes inside me, the ones whose beauty stays stable
& the ones whose materials age into abject stature, shit-colored &
stiff with degraded latex or rubber. I kin with her contingencies it
pains me to leave /

                                tremendous new feelings although there are
confusions / they are strong black white none gray

        I have a headache in a burning house for years

Sitting up in bed I write

                              a long sharp stitch hard as a wooden ruler
in my side. I make measure, take measure, lines as long as thought,
stopped short –

                    this much pain

                    now this much

I love deixis
& especially how it fails when I write *this* pain & *this* & *this here now
now now*, the seconds a series of soft boxes, the lyric a collapsed
calendar, the day a ruin without rue for a little while. "Only joyful
discoveries count," says Agnes, these minutes I can't remember,
fragments of clarity precise in pencil

                    new & being discovered at the same time

          touching in its fragility

                                        about labor & skill

an illegible hand turns writing to drawing.
When I write *clarity* & *precise*, it doesn't mean I can read them. I read
past them into time, a book of paintings open on the blue bedspread,
the notebook in my lap. "Find an object," Johns says, "Invent a
function." I feel the ruler click against my ribs, pain the exact sound
of beads on an abacus measuring

                    one thing working one way
          another   "   "   another   "

                    One thing working different ways
                    <u>at different times</u>

for C. D. Wright & Jean Valentine

Problem : body : problem : space : problem : time :

problems
that extend to language & money. The notebook allows me to be
private in public

writing on the bus or in the waiting room

time flows toward a destination in space

next stop my name an
open door. In Antje's office courtesy of a sliding scale I lie down on
the couch & look out: blue sky above a turquoise wall, a little
treatise on color theory. I believe, as Agnes says, "Anything can be
painted without representation," & in some sessions we don't talk
much

inside our wordlessness a shared color

sometimes a memory,
sometimes a mood. C. D. tells me our friend Jean reminds her of
Agnes. "Gray is the intermediate state she inhabits with no apparent
effort," she writes, "In the gray space, the spirit starts to find shape,
to find internal structure." The point – it doesn't exist in this world
& some of her poems capture it, fine gradations between *grey* with
an *e* & *gray* with an *a*. Maybe because of Antje's window

our shared color

a shade of blue

a field of borage flooding the room. & sometimes
white, strangely painful when we tense to the unsaid. Intimate like
washing an egg fallen from a nest. To speak would break a thread
of red into a bone cup.

Love's a misreading that can be borne – until it can't. When a friend finds Agnes in a psychotic state on the street, she ends up in Bellevue. Some say it's brought about by her relationship with the artist Lenore Tawney; some say it's just part of a long pattern of psychotic breaks; after it she leaves Manhattan for good, 1967. Critics at the time see parallels between Tawney's work on the loom & Agnes' grids that "might be the design for a woven fabric." – Oh don't give me that, she says later, Somebody undercutting me, saying it's like weaving

translucency & tremolo

there is an ethic
in the color made

by the hand

that put quietness
inside me

Agnes titles some
of Tawney's earliest woven forms; Tawney titles pieces hung while Agnes is hospitalized, titles she complains about in 1973 as "*romantic* not *classic* & a contradiction of the work," her later grievance as acute as her earlier attachment. "It can be said that trembling & sensitive images are as though brought before our eyes as we look at them," Agnes writes in 1961 of Tawney's weavings, "& also that deep, & sometimes dark & unrealized feelings are stirred in us

there is penetration

an urgency that sweeps us up

it is going to be like the waves

over & over again   forever

is not too long   for the real thing

After we watch *Wanda*, I return to it over & over, haunted by the heaviness it leaves in my body. Insistent without words, indefinitely somatic, the film remembers for me

what it means to be from "nowhere," a place abandoned by the culture / to be a person abandoned of place of origin & class & gender / to be a person dependent on a beloved & abusive figure / to be loved, you believe their negating vision of you *is* you / to survive you're forced to confuse your identity

with theirs. *Why can't you do right?* my mother asks, sending a scant check for me & my "friend" to visit. I haven't been back in a decade & don't want to go, but R's moved by filial piety. After she agrees to "allow" us to sleep in the same room, we stay for three days

on her best behavior, hair in curlers beneath a pert scarf. She refuses meals & won't leave the house except for church. She starts drinking early afternoons while she eats Fritos & beats us at poker, then retreats, passing out each night in bed, TV on. It's hard to watch

Loden as Wanda & I can't stop. Into her wide, angular face the film collapses the ways our culture abjects the South, the white working class & women – & refuses anything that might suggest her life can turn out otherwise. Faced with Loden's uncompromising negation of American uplift, Pauline Kael opts for insult, calling Wanda a "sad, ignorant slut" & claiming her "small voice, her helplessness – are too minor & muted for a full-length film." My family too

my mother withdrawing into herself so long ago I confuse every subsequent refusal with her. R & I lie awake in my childhood bed among the pines I love & listen. On the one hand, their tall straight trunks creaking in wind. On the other, her unkempt house, its heavy weather of neglect. R holds my hand & says: I think I get it now. I think I understand where you're coming from.

Johns loves an R / I love an R. When Johns & R break up, it's with admirable severity & what follows are years of the work I like best. A fine gray seething

grievance / then radical extravagance. When R tells me not to write about him, I try to obey without understanding how. There are so many things I can't do of my own volition

can't sleep

faster / dream more quickly

`

can't mend my relationship to the real without writing. Then I what. Try to cut him from the notebook the way a heartbroken lover might cut an ex out of old photos

I can't cut him out entirely. He stands just outside the sightline of each line. I have to wait. The right words arrive through their own relation to time. Such is the manner of our seeing. Such the conditions of our love.

This page is for Jay DeFeo. After dental work she can barely afford even with cash from teaching extra classes, she takes the bridge out of her mouth & paints it – "my model / out of my own head!" – a landscape like the Oakland hills, stunned cluster of late summer blackberries. The canvases look like September smells at night, dry grasses gold in the dark, fine yellow dust sifting up from my steps. What I like best

> the construct-
> destruct feature

> from abstract
> to representation

> no one can say
> moved linearly

> (or

the first chance
to see a Johns retrospective I decline. Instead I spend afternoons in the DeFeo show hung opposite his. Alone with *The Rose* I bask in its auratic stature & want to stay with Jay, who toughs out years of poverty, bad teeth, worse luck, sexism & her own character. Eight years of paint, stellar rays troweled into thousands of pounds of stony glow spiked with mica: I let them comfort me. Somehow she draws even in hospice, swinging as always between monumental & microscopic, her final still lifes a pink ceramic cup. A friend's gift. The work like the life

> not perfection

> but the inevitable

> form of the idea

The insularity of illness. Outside: a smoker's laugh heavy, wet with phlegm. Passersby talk to their small dogs beneath the plaza's tall palms. What I too often leave out: I'm sick in a city, a neighborhood busy with buses guided by wires like this sentence between printed lines. Overhead they hum a little song, ping & spark. By the bus stop sparrows seek the seeds an elder scatters every day from a bread bag on his lap. Here

> I dream a bite on my wrist doesn't heal.
> "   "   beetles pour forth from my mouth.
> "   "   I shit blood in a paper cup

in bed, in the thrift store chair,
on the couch, in a different chair in the same room, from general to specific, the way sleep moves, on scraps of paper, on a laptop, in the notebook, I write & leave almost everything out, I think, to empty the form illness makes of my life. In this way days pass like pages blown from the same broken spine

Unreal City

What shall we ever do?

a busted cardboard box
of books down the block. "The resistance modernity offers to the individual," Benjamin suggests, "is out of all proportion to his [sic] strength." SROs crowned with pigeon spikes, facades dwarfed by sky, I write, a city seized by what moves it, blue blurring into haze, stratospheric white. Not water. Not wind. Not the wind that precedes wildfires. What is this other weather in me.

Rain gray as graphite falls, fine powder staining the day. These minutes on the bus are the most I feel like a *we*, warm jackets pressing in on either side. At the clinic I take a number, individual again on a hard folding chair. The anticipation of meaning, being in the waiting room like being at the museum, "the mood of keeping your eyes open & looking." This notebook, costume of making do, getting by

One system laid over another

synecdoche for the body: beige wool unravelling sweater hem, green worn shiny corduroy elbow, pink skirt with a period stain nearly hidden by pleats.

In certain areas the information in one system
matches the information in the other

or

red umbrella a patient shakes out in the vestibule. Door open, spatter pattern. A wet black pigeon struts into the waiting room

Two kinds of space
can, in part, be one kind of space

without touch or test, the doctor offers a misdiagnosis, a useless prescription I can't afford. Out of pocket? Fuck it. "One wants from painting a sense of life," Johns says. Whose life, which part of it. "It has to be what you can't avoid saying." Failed by another, I leave the room a failure. "Not a deliberate statement but a helpless statement." My bank statement.

Overdrawn on the 11th of the month. The check from the college comes late, with a note not to cash it for two weeks. Hand to mouth, I laugh as I cash it. Then checks stop coming. The administration asks us to continue teaching as they sell off assets

classroom
space / our slim salaries

vanish into venture capital & the rumor of recession. In the notebook, the pressures that come to bear on the margins constrain, frame each sentence

Shake (shift) parts
of some

A not complete unit
or a new unit.

"Pure" writing's impossible. Why not incorporate scratches & fragments left by the contexts in which we suffer from having been being

our unhandsome condition an index
of injury

Avoid the idea of a puzzle
that could be solved

FLAG, 1954-55 (II)

Encaustic, oil & collage on fabric mounted on wood (3 panels)
41 ¼ x 60 ¾ inches

to johns i write   *a faggot has no true flag*   as if his painting   a simulacrum

on a bedsheet   in layers of newspaper   dipped in hot wax   *could be* a true flag

i know it's not   + not *not* a flag   the way a faggot's not a man   + not *not* a man

i hate his archive   but i like this snapshot of him   just two years out of the army

crouching beneath this painting   in 1955   pale & boyish   former soldier

the historian calls   *a docile body*   object & target of power   johns says he dreamt

of painting this   a fact art critics repeat   without asking why   the historian

calls the soldier's body   *a fragment of mobile space*   as if war were just collage

soldier cut out of context   pasted into another   like *time*'s man of the year

in 1951   "name: american"   "occupation: fighting man"   johns is drafted

works on graphic design in japan   while soldiers & civilians   millions   die

in korea   & now here he is   in a new york loft   his boyfriend behind the camera

saucepans & hot plate on the floor   white mound of beeswax   to make encaustic

for eight more stars   each detail   part of a political anatomy   still unfinished

Language feels social but the green is wrong & the white is wrong
& sentences end the way I begin a food journal to track my reactions
& lose interest quick: everything makes me sick. Not a figure of
speech. I *literally* can't. I admire the way Agnes trusts painting to
represent what seems impossible on this earth

                                                    Perhaps fragment
                                                    it so that
                                                    its own work
                                                    its own
                                                    its
                                                    legibility is interfered
                                                    with

the confusion of nausea & self-hatred / Color
continues its essentially private experience within a semiotic
system. A moment yellow like the shame after vomiting. In that
respect, I'm like Johns who in the early 60s reads Wittgenstein's
On Certainty. "I do not know how the sentence 'I have a body' is to
be used," writes Ludwig, a sentence I underline in my twenties.
Now I think, Oh grow up, gay. *It uses you*

                                                    Entities
                                                    ————————
                                                    splitting

self into symptoms, synesthesia, site
of intense intimacies: facial flushing, sweating, heat rash, fatigue. I
fall asleep in the green of figs during a conversation with my friend
Miranda, in a meaty violet in the middle of an argument with R.
Illness is a relationship, serious & mortal. I never choose to be in it

                                        – & neither does he.

No worst, there is none

                                            & I'm it, trailing shit. Some days
pitched past pitch of grief I can't leave the flat where I double
over, nausea's fore-pangs scoring the hours before the wilder
wringing out. Then my cries heave woe, world-sorrow, then lull,
leaving one comfort: an empty gut. Each time I feel in all my gall
& heartburn the fell of dark flat as the book left face-down on the
bed

        The act of taking food.

        The act of preparing
        & taking food
        & over that

        black or dark wash

                                            in the cool white
quiet of museum rooms in voiceover. *You have to go where you have
the most clarity*, Kiki Smith says. Where's that. Down on all fours
on the gallery floor. I love the creeping figure when I see her:
ruddy wretch, ass spattered with crap, her absurd long turd
telling shame a tail. Sister with beeswax skin, papier-mâché
stranger, sweating self, with her as my witness: where I write
days, I mean *years*, mean *life*. But worse. Oh yes, there is one –

What's the event that bisects a biography, after which nothing is the same. What's the shape of the moment when you lose everything *except* your life. Double negative, skull against canvas. The emergency's so big my mind can't hold it. Corpse & mirror, a duet. I wake up in a hard bleached bed a debtor. Then I what. Ask another artist afterward: how do I do this?

writing or painting   as a way of writing

or painting   or as a way of doing something else

another possibility   *way* can be used to mean

this is the way I do this   this is the way he does this

this is the way he does it   I do it this way

The emergency's so big my body can't hold it. I need to build a structure it can live in. Lead section. Bronze junk. Glove. Glass. Brush. <u>Dark</u> glass ⟶ mouth. It swallows everything. I follow the taste of salt, thinking until the ambulance arrives. "What's that even mean," I hear myself saying to the EMT. Someone pulls a curtain across it. This wordless event that never ends.

All my strengths turn against me. Decisive & unwavering when well, I really don't know how to be ill. In meditation, in analysis, in book after book – I seek the right way to suffer as if it were a problem I could solve, blocked by stubborn wrong thought & circumstance. Migraine holds my brain in a white cup. Into the same bowl I scrub I throw up

> hair

> dried blood color

> art materials

> & food

in bed I let each thought click
bead after bead on a bone abacus: occipital, cervical, thoracic, lumbar, sacral. "But helplessness when fear & dread have run their course, as all passions do," Agnes writes, "is the most rewarding state of all." What bullshit. Years pass in the dark like the bus beeping at the corner as it kneels, sound that means *home*. I don't want to leave. Each notebook sentence as it is, was, might be ⟵⟶
A through Z, not a structure ⟵⟶ not a construction

> but if it were

> all would be

> described &

> swallowed up

after the emergency
memory begins again behind a privacy curtain. Esophagus raw, each minute I spend here is literal money, the single tense in which I live. I hear a distant distraught man weeping. I can't sleep thinking what <u>this</u> costs.

How did I get here? What I too often leave out: I'm sick among people. Not unlike Johns in documentary footage, intent on the etching plate in the midst of a busy studio, I am at work, pain this tricky spot, his little brush dabbing at it.

                                        a tendency here

                                        to involve the eye & the arm

/ you're in a healing crisis," says Miranda
then the doctor's awkward small talk before the rectal exam, his
receptionist saying "We'll bill you." Even then, even in debt, the
genuine, the miraculous, vocative. Being

                                        called into being
                                        in certain areas

                                        one figure becomes the ground
                                        for the other figure

how I say "I'm broke," & Antje asks
"You're broken?" Paint can't do that, the rough voice of the nurse
saying hello when I wake up. "Aim for maximum difficulty," writes
Johns, "in determining what has happened." If biography doesn't
take care of that. Hospital white. It's all so interesting, I forget to
cry.

Migraine leaks a fecal stain into the look of things, fatigue changes the pressure & weight of them on skin. What I can't remember doesn't leave me. I build this little failure for it, something that can be erased or shifted, distorted as a shadow, perhaps on falling. Stretcher or part of chair

                              bolt, hinge / or

hinge / here ———⟶   IF
                      the body were oiled   what kind

                      Step onto a canvas

                      Prone
                      Up

this canvas could
then be dropped – to rest on the floor. After R says, "Don't write about me," I notice neither Agnes nor Johns allow talk about biography. Her psychotic breaks, his bitter breakup, their queerness. If *Adventure* were a grid,

                                        if *Fool's House*
were oil on canvas with objects –

                        if I could gather loss under a title:
Poem Bitten by a Man.

                "Because the body doesn't speak in systems of power," Daphne Marlatt writes," "its 'speaking' . . . breaks out through the codes that repress it." The notebook open to catch a signal, what I'm writing for. Distressed surface, an infinity of language, some clear souvenir.

In her writings, Agnes is declarative. In his sketchbooks, Johns is interrogative. Both offer instruction, but Johns talks only to himself. "Remove the signs of 'thought'," he writes in 1968, "It is not the 'thought' which needs showing." He uses scare quotes to mark an idea whose meaning or value remains under suspicion & a question to mark a site of inquiry. She never uses either, though in the documentary she does mark the necessity of getting rid of ideas entirely to ready her mind for inspiration. To friends, she describes "pushing back the voices in her head to find the silence." To be ill, low income, uninsured & receive health care, I *have* to have ideas. I have to prove to bureaucrats I deserve care. I think of Agnes' delight in an empty mind while I fill out forms & offer triplicate copies of qualifying documents. "I had a hard time giving up evolution & the atomic theory," Agnes says, laughing, "but I managed it, so I don't believe in either

/ the condition of a presence

knee   leg   torso   feet

the condition of being here

Vibrant life

detail from *détailler*

"to cut to pieces"

relation
stops nowhere. Sitting in the public health clinic waiting room I feel
acute tenderness again toward *us*, the endless *now* in which we ask
for help. Advice about child care, unzipped fly, cute bag beyond
gender, ashy elbows, flirty banter, purple walker decorated with
rhinestones

the surface
of waiting appears to pulse

a chain of objects

a geometry of its
own

can painting do this? this feeling of collectivity that blunts the
cuts the State makes between people, people & services, people &
their own agency, the number each of us takes in the name of care.
I want to make the number that means each of us gets the care we
need

whether or not we can "prove" we "deserve" it

I want to
make a shape

Something that has no name

to take across the
threshold from *we* to *I* / a shape to protect from medicine's terrible
arrogance in the examination room.

The way an abstract canvas relates to its title, what language does.
X-rays & bloodwork, a grid called *Tree*, this surprise hospital bill
for $24,000.00. Choosing making, I choose how to continue to live

believing painting

to be a language

there seems to be a "pressure area" "underneath"

after the emergency
I find comfort in the wisdom figure Agnes makes of herself, a role
Johns assiduously avoids. I'm consoled by grids that for her
represent innocence, her writing's dogmatic certainties & even her
famous provocation that the wiggle of an earthworm is more
important than the assassination of a president, a politics I find
indefensible. In this respect she & Johns sometimes resemble each
other. "in a context / within a context," writes Johns, "to what degree
movable

/ I arrive at every moment undiagnosed

language which operates in such a way as to force
the language to change

toward new recognitions

the wordless event of which any visual form is evidence

I just don't want anything expensive to happen. After the college closes & its real estate sells, I queue with former colleagues in the halls of the labor board's big glass building to file a claim for back wages. In need of a salary & time to write & health insurance, I'm "awarded" wages I've already earned. They never arrive. When I return to complain, the state worker says there's nothing they can do. "You should lawyer up

                                   Whether to see the 2 parts as one thing

                                       or as two things   Another possibility:

                                   to see that something has happened

like the unsolicited advice
healthy people give about "wellness." Have you considered endocrine burnout? depression? low testosterone? leaky gut? Have you tried a juice cleanse? colonics? suppositories? an elimination diet? How about supplements? bone broth? collagen? these herbs? this tincture? What about an exercise regimen? pilates? mindful breathing? guided meditation? crystals? singing bowls? reiki? How about journaling? Have you ever tried to write about it?

Quoting is biting & I am so hungry, the notebook

———▶ mouth

mouth   mouth

full of phrases I've taken between my teeth. "The satisfaction of appetite is frustrating," Agnes writes, "It's always better to be a little bit hungry." I lie in bed in a recursive loop of crises. For how many years does the recession begin, the college close? For how long do I endure emergency? On how many days without pay or health insurance do bills arrive & late fees & then – fear. "I've never known someone who complains so much," R says

<u>ways of putting things together</u>

Not a logical system
That is, not contained

continuity / discontinuity

the object serves
to mend the damage done by loving's intrinsic aggression. "I can remember the minute I was born," Agnes says in the documentary, "I thought I was quite a small figure with a little sword." The object also serves to build up the strength to tolerate the destructiveness inside one's own loving. "& I thought I was going to cut my way through life with my little sword." For a long time I lie in crisis. Even forbidden the act of mending, I'm still certain. "Victory after victory," I'm going to do it.

I wake to a mind somehow as precise as *On a Clear Day*: thirty screenprints, twelve by twelve, black ink on white rag paper, each image a variant of the grid. "Hold your mind as empty & tranquil as they are," Agnes advises, "& recognize your feelings at the same time." I take the bus to Bernal Heights & walk to the hilltop over the city. I feel my small life caught far below, a raptor eye fixed on it.

"Now I see making contexts for my objects as a scene for making concepts," Lauren Berlant writes, "which requires a creative archival practice, a construction of objects from the currents among collected things." & there's an ethical tension between people & things as they are & how they live inside us. Antje suggests feeling failed is proportional to feeling attached. Objects inside me are charged, hot to the touch, & they're also not objects at all – real & historical lives, independent of mine

the superimposition
of 2 not quite
identical images

2 things occupying
the same space

(a fist & a hand

Dying of breast cancer, Loden
talks about her mother, who tries to abort her & then, after divorcing her father, asks her grandparents to raise her. In documentary footage, Loden relates how she leaves North Carolina at sixteen & stays estranged until her mother needs caregiving. They reconcile just before she dies. "I feel my mother still lives through me," Loden says, "& through what I do, I might be able to help to express some of the things my mother wasn't able to express in her lifetime." Like *Wanda*

is every beloved object also one's mother? On the phone she says: *You better not lose your friend. You'll never find anyone else who'd put up with you.*

I keep trying to get better. Illness is a rival worse to R than writing, a more complete withdrawal. In a dark room I sit the migraine straight-spined on a zafu. In a dark room the healer Marintha, a friend of Miranda's, inserts needles into my skin & heat peels off my body like steam from a cup of tea. In a dark room cool colors crowd the silence between Antje & me. What else can I do but acknowledge & let go

healing without cure

each thought like an
aesthetic gesture that outlives its historical context. Though it appears repetitive, illness is serial, a project in which

in each room
/ on each page

embodiment starts as disequilibrium & each
time travels differently through the material until it's as specific & particular as any minute of any day. What I can't do

experience
what is temporary

illness might not be. Each symptom, each pain,
promises in the moment their permanence & my mind lurches into a future where each hurts worse. Irregular, inexact, each line in the notebook calls attention to itself without giving direct access to skin. In a dark room the nest of worked nerves that crowns my head stings

each line
singular

a circuit of vervain. Lobed & toothed,
spiked with mauve blooms opening, this is prescribed for what I think, my mind the scald the hot cup holds.

From the sickbed where I seethe with grievance, *invalid* & *invalid*
look the same

                                        a saturating body
                that makes the whole assemblage flow away & breaks
                                        the symbolic structure

here where I'm not writing about R
I find a new hierarchy of passions in the minor literature written
by the ill: cool side of the pillow, folded blanket behind the knees
to ease the sacrum, ice pack on the head, lights out & curtains
drawn. The migraine

                        a plaster negative of a whole head.

                        a rubber positive of this.

                        cut & (stretched) laid on a board fairly flatly.

                        cast in bronze & titled <u>Skin</u>

with object-like opacity
R lists all the things I can no longer do. He says he thinks of me now
not as ill but as disabled. He says his desire's blocked, cut off from all
its connections. He uses against me my own body

                                        "unfuckable"
                                        "unreasonable"
                                        "unlovable"

is what I hear from across the kitchen table
/ He describes his place for me within love's major language: my
presence political, hostile, an impasse. He violently others me in
my own home! Then I what.

                                Invalid in this sentence I kneel
& harsh the toilet with bristles. *Invalid* in this sentence I shove my
gloved hand into the shitty fixture of literature & scrub it.

Welcome to the spring of the word *precarity*, job interviews in
borrowed clothes. My mouth holds evidence of recession. I show
the bourgeoisie my low-income grin to convince them I'm worth
more than bleeding gums. *Committee* rhymes with *pity*. Suffering
from a political system hostile to care, hostile to art, I run into
Miranda on the street. She asks how I am & I cry

> exposure of layers
> (thing)
> (2 things)
>
> what are techniques
> for recognition
>
> for exposing
> the lower layer

grateful & embarrassed by my need to be seen
without antagonism. "Do you personally feel you owe something
to a society that's willing to pay you so much for your work?" an
interviewer asks Johns in 1989. After Reagan guts public health &
welfare. After Johns' paintings begin to earn millions at auction
"To what degree is a society involved?" he asks. "Indebted? I don't
think so."

> "stupid as a painter" Duchamp
> "jealous as an artist" Flaubert

I walk with R
to the public health clinic, the first appointment he's come to. The
doctor says I've run out of available tests, offers psychiatric meds as
if it's all in my head. Why does the State lay blame on the people it
fails? *Why am I always with crazy people?* R asks after we leave. As if
I'm not there.

> Q: Is this where we part ways? A: Outside the clinic
door I take a different route home, avoiding our spot in Dolores
Park, an empty hilltop bench. Then I what. Tear up the fucking
script. I get rid of everything.

Broom

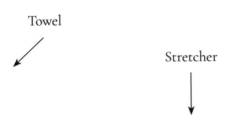

Towel

Stretcher

Cup

FLAG ABOVE WHITE WITH COLLAGE, 1955

Encaustic & collage on canvas
22 x 19 inches

forty-eight scars   part of a political anatomy   still unfinished   in the 1950s

the critic writes   modern art keeps getting entangled   in america's contradictions

but what doesn't   in any american era   i'm an analysand   in my anxiety dream

about the flag paintings   the analyst says *don't worry*   *paintings also have an unconscious*

structured as a language   produced in the social field   out of a historical situation

some read his deadpan flags   as "decadent" rejections   of the "heroic" AbEx paintings

the CIA sends around the globe   to combat socialist realism   *i intuitively like to paint flags*

johns tells *newsweek* in '58   *i have no ideas   about what the paintings   imply about the world*

EVERY AMERICAN FLAG   writes navajo artist demian dinéyazhí   IS A WARNING SIGN

from 1958-59   this painting tours the country   in a show called   *collage in america*

in it a white man   in a strip of photo-booth pictures   johns finds on the street

looks out from behind stripes   stretching past an uneven field   of battered stars

i imagine him   in davenport   nashville   tallahassee   laramie   poughkeepsie

a stranger   a watchman   passing through   his looking   looks back at our looking

Above the hotel room toilet, a muddy reproduction of *Target*, 1958, oil & collage on canvas. As I piss, I look at it, kind of a joke about men & their aim. How easily the image passes into the vernacular proves Johns right: "Anything can be used in some other way. Things aren't necessarily what we say they are or what we want them to be." The hotel's a block from the art school he attends for three semesters before he leaves Columbia for Manhattan, 1949. Catbirds cry in low-branched oaks shading the sidewalks.

Focus –

Include one's looking.
"   "   seeing.
"   "   using

it & its use &
its action

to hide in plain sight
/ I want to say it's a queer compositional strategy, a survival tactic born of the Cold War when "perverts" are public enemies, a *hominterm* "seducing & enervating the body politic." When there are elements of things seen in even the most abstracted impression, "Autobiography isn't necessarily an exposure of feelings," Johns says. I want to say it's "a way to allegorize social relations through a playing out of formal relations," as David Getsy writes. I want to say what looks like a delicate construct of compromise – ambiguity, code, open secret – is privacy. I want to say it leaves both the artist & the object more free.

My life is in disorder. I leave the hotel bed & walk the broad boulevards of the downtown grid. A grant's funding three days of research here, more of a road trip really, & *I am unable to will it to order* like dubious history, the way some narratives of South Carolina go heavy on the Revolution & light on centuries of enslavement before secession & the Confederacy. I sit atop the Capital steps at sunset, pot smoke wafting up from a couple on a date. My friend Tom texts: "get real. ur breaking up w/r." From this distance it doesn't seem like it. The emergency's changed everything that *makes sense of my life, would bring it to order, interpreting as I go*

     this is a message

     from the half

     in the sky

           that Rilke poem everyone loves that ends *You must change your life.* Do they also love how he abandons his wife Clara – a sculptor & painter – & his daughter Ruth to write in a castle paid for by patrons? "There is no choice while we are on the true path," Agnes writes, "Disobedience is unhappiness." After she leaves New York, she seems to give up on intimacy. "Let's not be friends," she writes after a visitor leaves New Mexico. I can't forgive myself that I cause R pain, even as he causes me pain. It feels like it will feel like this forever, a standoff between conscience & grievance. I know it *appears stable but is not.* I'm afraid it will never end; I'm afraid it will

             this is a message

             from the other half

             in the sea

The way I take an eraser to the page until it begins to pill & tear: nothing feels right except how I make of paper my disappearance. In the hotel bed again I watch Agnes paint, answering questions as she applies watery acrylic with a small brush. Like the documentarian, I want something from her, this color I perceive as pink she says is red

> & no two people alike
> or any moment of their lives.

I don't *choose* abstraction.
It's one thing to pursue selflessness, another to vanish against your will. "I am nothing absolutely," Agnes writes, "There is this other thing going on." They don't seem to be sentences about derealization or illness, but that's how I hear them, busy with symptoms & metaphysics. "I have tried existing & I do not like it," she writes to a friend, "I have decided to give it up." Some continue to seek her out in the desert as though she is a sage, all adobe & aphorisms

> *you just can't be an artist*

> she says to the camera

> *if you can't be alone*

psychosis
catatonia, aural hallucinations – ideas about herself she doesn't have. "I'm not a woman," she insists, "I'm a doorknob!" Trances, visions, voices, are her preferred terms. "I do not think there will be any more people in my life," she writes in a letter, "Do not think that that is sad. It is not sad. Even sadness is not sad." White queer mad woman of a certain age – one way to describe her. "A great woman," as Jill Johnston writes after a visit, is another way. I dream I leave a smooth oval stone on the page I've erased, cairn to mark my way along a path I can no longer see.

What's erased returns as color I can't remember, can't bear to experience. This wordlessness mothers everything unspoken, everything unsaid or unsayable true as a bruise on the palest part of my inner arm. Time can't survive inside it, where my eye & ear & tongue & skin consume the same surface

                                                    / a mother
has to be able to tolerate

                        hating her baby," Winnicott writes, "without doing anything about it."

                        "God how she hated me," Agnes says. She remembers her mother locks her two- & three-year old self outside *so she won't have to look at her*. Johns never speaks about it publicly, but his cousin Mary Young reports that his mother abandons Johns so young because, divorced & unable to care for him, *she didn't want to keep it*. After my father's vasectomy fails, I'm an accident, object of antagonism from the start: my mother restricts calories so effectively, she brags, she gains just nine pounds more than my birth weight

                                            instead of solid bodies

                    bodies capable of being

                                converted to color

/ who taught your mother
to love like that?" Antje asks. I never find out. & I never love Agnes more than when she describes her newborn self as a little figure with a sword. "Everybody is born 100% ego," she says next, "& after that it's just adjustment."

[57]

"I adjusted as soon as they carried me into my mother," she says, laughing, "Half of my victories fell to the ground. My mother had the victories." In bed I watch this speech again & think about her psychotic episodes, so like "primitive agonies" an infant experiences when care fails

> Return to an unintegrated state.
> Falling forever.
> Loss of sense of real.
> Loss of capacity to relate to objects.

I open the notebook.
Poíēsis : to make an object / to mend a psychic rupture with the world / to order a disordered relation to the past where sentimentality is useless, a denial of hate, a matter on which R & I disagree. He's quick to anger & quickly forgives, whereas when wordlessness fills me I'm hidden

inside a rack of fabric samples in the craft store. First conscious memory: bliss until my mother leaves, drives off for so long that, when she returns, I've lapsed into a dry, quiet ire so private I remain hidden even from myself / preserving my love for those I hate / who make me who I am

without whom I would continue falling forgotten into color forever

perhaps like Johns after his parents' divorce. From the age of two he's raised by his grandfather William Isaac & his second wife Montez & then, after W. I. dies, by his aunt Gladys. "From early childhood," Johns says, "I was always going to be an artist." Then he what. Makes, as he writes in his sketchbook

> an object that tells
> of the loss, destruction,
> disappearance of objects.
> Does not speak of
> itself. Tells of
> others. Will it
> include them?
> DELUGE

A freight train passes through the frame into this sentence, childhood nights I think its mournful horn is the sound the horizon makes when the sun sets behind it. The camera waits on Main St., at the railroad crossing in Allendale, the small South Carolina town where Johns is a kid. "Everything I do is attached to my childhood," he says, "It wasn't especially cheerful." Of the extent to which I use the language of others as an approximation of my own, I write

Shifting the facts

Move the frame (or the canvas)

A rearrangement

unmown baseball field
fireworks emporium, all the signage unchanged since Allendale last had money. I sense the documentarians looking for a person who doesn't seem to appear in the work. I watch this brief interlude several times – rural like where I grow up after my father takes a job in Alabama. Economic migrants, we're some kind of white, different than the locals. When a classmate calls us "carpetbaggers," I dig through photos taken in homes rented or bought with work in Indiana, Missouri, Kansas, Virginia, Georgia

/ Q: Where I'm *really* from?

A: I recognize this filmstock, the same washed-out pastels of snapshots from our early years in Alabama, grainy azaleas just thrust in the dirt. I pause the image at the crossing to gaze up at the peculiar Polaroid powder blue that will always look like the 80s. Sky a thin skin of polymers across the color line.

There's a kind of white that's more than white

critical discourse
about Johns is that kind of white. A white not created by bleach but
that is itself bleach, the way the documentarians refuse to
acknowledge filming in a majority Black town. "A black sense
of place," Katherine McKittrick argues, "draws attention to
geographic processes that emerged from plantation slavery & its
attendant racial violence yet cannot be contained by the logics
of white supremacy." It's why most critics don't know what to do
about Johns' relation to the South except to place it in bleach
repeatedly

?
How does the (eye) make such distinctions

↓

Linguistically, perhaps, the verb is important

But what about such a case in painting?

visual virtuosity

in Allendale
on its one intact downtown block. No one's out on the street. Too
hot, even in shade across from the former train station, even in the
notebook, a nauseous blot of ink made by sweat ╲

↘

crepe myrtle & Spanish moss.
The pictorial tends to betray
the South. What am I looking for? Seat of a county W. I. Johns helps
found in 1919, a place some white folks remember as "the best that
could be desired." The old Johns manse on Main gone for decades,
though its floorplan lives on in his paintings. *The Town of Allendale*
doesn't say what Black folks remember despite being 86% of the
population.

Allendale's founded on cotton; Johns' early life is funded by it. The front page of the August 6th, 1925 edition of the *Barnwell People-Sentinel* devotes ample column space to news of the crop, noting "Allendale Man Ships 1st Bale / W. I. Johns Grows Early Cotton This Year. / Two Bales of Fleecy Staple Ginned & Shipped from Allendale Last Thursday. / It is said he broke all records in this State for early shipment, this being the first time in history that new crop cotton has been shipping from South Carolina in July." His white is *that*

        kind of white

            which suggests "the world"

            which suggests "things which are"

            the most conventional thing
            the most ordinary thing –

                they exist as clear facts

                                  / a black
sense of place is not a standpoint or a situated knowledge," McKittrick writes, "it is a location of difficult encounter & relationality." In the critical discourse about Johns, you mostly have to go to endnotes to locate that encounter, as if to talk about Johns & race you have to *enter around back*: "[21] As a Southerner in the state that was first to secede from the Union, Johns remembers talk about the Civil War that was still within living memory & has related childhood stories of growing up in a racially divided community; Bernstein journal, July 24 2006." Like his sexuality, race is not something Johns talks about in public. I'm raised to believe this is "just" good manners.

A wound is a mood

                if it doesn't heal, it lasts a lifetime, like childhood or history, & occupies a body absolutely. In the 70s, I-95 reroutes tourists forty miles east & amenities along Route 301 through town go bust, motels & restaurants of the motor age. Then the textile mills go overseas. The peeling Lobster House sign still presides over the abandoned parking lots of rural depopulation, -20% since the last census. Emptied buildings scoured by what Christina Sharpe calls *the weather of the wake.* "It is not the specifics of any one event or set of events that are endlessly repeatable & repeated," she writes, "but the totality of the environments in which we struggle." Under cloudless sky I pause this time in person, white body at the crossing

                        Something which has a name

                        Something which has no name

                        One thing made of another

                        Try to use together

                                the walls
                                the layers
                                the mouth
                                & the teeth

/ absolutely art-free"
Johns says, "Therefore I had to go far away, to a different, interesting world." White artists from the rural South, especially gay ones, often sound like him, the way white Southerners who stay often sound like his cousin Mary, talking in voiceover about the 1930s: "Back there when Jasper was here, it was such a small town. You went out to play & didn't have to say where you were going because everybody took care of you." It's a white memory, thick presence of a naked, self-obscuring body of history. I know where we are, Jim Crow.

Back there when, W. I. Johns is "a prosperous farmer," another voiceover states. *Grandaddy*, Mary says. Born on a Bamberg County plantation in 1869, son & nephew of Confederate soldiers, he grows up to own 7,000 acres, "one of the largest cotton producers in South Carolina," reports the *History* of the state in 1920, erasing the Black laborers who make the land & produce his wealth. "Somewhere in Johns' fraught Southern body & work," writes Ralph Lemon, "is the abject horror of the Jim Crow South & all that came before

/ *What is it that work reveals*, asks Johns, *Work reveals itself really.* & his style depends on the kinds of space he neglects to recognize, reinscribing, as McKittrick writes, "the violence that often accompanies the production of space

/ *Neutrality must involve some relationship*,

Johns writes,

"Neutral" expresses an intention

later in the documentary
White Flag at auction sells for 6.4 million dollars, a record until *False Start* sells for 17.5 million the following day. Lemon argues John's paintings can be so highly valued precisely because they don't refer to the Black suffering & exploitation an earlier generation of Johns fights to sustain & which support him for a while as a sort-of-orphan, too fey for his estranged father. Abstraction offers mobility only to some: Johns is free to leave & return two decades later to work in a house in Edisto Beach he buys with his fame. "Why disrupt one's inherent freedom," Lemon asks, "by being fully seen?"

The land outside this sentence is flat, the soil sandy, what art can make or unmake, reveal or conceal, embedded anyway in context. "I paint with my back to the world," Agnes likes to say, still *in* the world. The documentarians include shots of the Johns family plot as if to prove something. Spanish moss above headstones, then *vine ripe tomatoes* painted by hand, Black Cat Fireworks, montage a home to what they leave unspoken: Allendale county's thirty six known plantations. Now I stand in the same live oak shade in the Swallow Savannah Cemetery outside town, history

> An accumulation of what
>
> An explosion   "   "
>
> An expulsion   "   "

& think of Agnes, born to homesteaders
settlers on Treaty 6 territory of the Cree, Assiniboine & Saulteaux nations, her memories of the plains of western Saskatchewan "so flat," she says, "you could see the curvature of the earth." In the high white light of noon I write this beneath a tall loblolly. I recognize from childhood the pine needles I sit on, umber & much longer than my fingers, their fascicles wrapped tightly in the same colonial history as my own. On film, three timber crosses rough as railroad ties mark the edge of the cemetery. Thirty years later they're still here, stark gray against green farmland beyond.

I think about Johns & me in our small towns. My parents share with rural Southerners an anxious, assimilationist surveillance of gender & the pitiless criticism of deviations from norms that facilitate white social mobility. To others I'm just "one of them Teare boys" until I'm *sissy* then *faggot*.

When a wealthy patron compliments the smooth good manners she assumes comes from Southern aristocracy, Johns says he's "just white trash," a quip I'm curious about. Geraldine Lewis, his father's one-time girlfriend, describes the young Johns as "sweet" & "always trying to please." For her, he embroiders flour sacks he's ripped open, bleached & hemmed into dishtowels, a gift for which his father calls him a sissy

/ a class of individuals defined by sexual preferences & practices," Didier Eribon writes, "also a set of processes of 'subjection' as much collective as individual

a common structure of inferiorization

/ a trap, a confinement.
The nature of the maze –

to follow a thread.
A way out, *the* way out

if the only way into the social
is insult. When I first encounter Agnes & Johns, I assume they make abstraction in part to escape, forbidding biography in order to bar insult from entering discourse around their work. I come to love the paradox of turning materiality (the painted space) into a release from materiality's trap

"In relation to everything that is given

/ who wouldn't want out
who wouldn't use the forces sent to destroy them for insight. I do & I don't. Then I what. *I'm still going outside*

The field's far edge bends, a trick of humidity, the blue of water hueing the air that seems to peel up off the green in waves. It hums like the place in my body cicadas make, a little sheet of copper the heat shakes. Maybe you have to be from here to hear it sing. "Land," Nikky Finney writes, "that Black folks made." The sound remains inside me, somatic as bone. Obliged to it for life, for more than I can write down now. A number of crops

cotton /

melons, asparagus, rye

his grandfather drives him to look at the fields. "He was a farmer. He would be very excited," Johns says, "& I couldn't understand how he could tell one thing from another." Patrimony's family plot: founding father whose son founders, dies young from drink, whose famous grandson surely won't be buried here. On a near grave someone's placed fake hydrangeas, plastic exuding the blue petals of acidic soil. Inside their history

I stand

a stranger

over graves on which I have no claim / I can touch
nothing

but what others leave behind

what I'm looking for

a link to the losses

that score the endless

pouring out of ourselves

into the world

Around cotton, the historian writes, "institutional, economic, racial, & political developments" fuse into one fate: *rural* means intimacy with the wake. White & not *not* Southern, I don't understand this until after I leave. Now I recognize the biased way white outsiders see the Deep South, *A vision of ruin, of decay, of utter emptiness – poor, neglected, hopeless-looking, a vivid failure*

Route 301: four lanes through pine & cropland, the road's width a reminder of decades when tourists cruise through to Florida. On occasion I pass another more or less neglected town, the inevitable rail running through. When I stop for gas the radio announces Sam Gilliam dies, Southern abstract painter the same generation as Johns.

/ *as though the colonizers had come & gone*, travel writer Paul Theroux writes of Allendale, *the settlers had bolted, most of the local people had fled*. It's pretty much what R says on his visit to Alabama, spooked by rural poverty, folks in trailers without septic hookups forced to pipe their shit into their own yards. Johns goes looking for Art as defined by a white Northern elite the way white outsiders come South expecting the colonizer's idealized pictorial landscape

Born in 1933 in Mississippi & raised in Kentucky, Gilliam moves in the early 60s to D. C. to paint. A decade later he archives himself: spattered coveralls, canvas, brushes, rollers, a paint tray, trowel, & other tools, all attached to a wood door he suspends a few inches above the floor. Hung in a gallery corner, it offers a situation a viewer enters on the cover of *The Washington Post*, a fur draped over one shoulder, 1973. She stands between the archive on display & a low platform that holds his worn work boots, one leaning gently toward the other. *Dark As I Am*, he calls it.

/ the landscape of the wake, the white sabotage of Reconstruction means *Every development problem I have ever witnessed in fifty years of traveling the world*, Theroux writes, *existed in Allendale*. In the notebook I pass the faded Black Cat Fireworks sign & turn down a pitted side street. Where vacant Victorians & shotgun shacks cave in on themselves, blackberry canes arc out of collapsed casements. Their white blossoms fizz with bees.

for Sam Gilliam

"You know, collage & assemblage have a great affinity with black artists, black people," Gilliam says about *Dark As I Am*, "To do this, even though it's just another side of what I'm doing with all the paintings, had a lot of meaning; had a lot of directness." That directness a rebuttal to critiques his abstractions aren't Black enough, political enough. He's dissatisfied with it

In the wake
with no state or nation to protect them, lifelong Black residents repeat the refrain, "There's nothing here. No jobs, high crime, nobody interested in helping," Patricia Johnson tells ABC News, "The things we ask for never come our way." Antiblackness is pervasive as climate, Sharpe writes, *The weather necessitates changeability & improvisation.*

/ & compresses the installation into a painting, an assemblage flattened onto a wood door that serves as support: clothing, backpack, painter's tools, wood closet pole. "Consider the way that individuated things or collections of such things," Fred Moten writes of Gilliam's work, "can be both medium & object of exchange." 87 x 47 x 3 ½ inches dripped with acrylic, a painting he calls *Composed (formerly Dark As I Am)*, the title yoking composition & composure – *com* + *posare*, "to place down together" – to identity's innate restlessness

"Our history says we're not a people who give up," council member Lottie Lewis says, "We fight." She leads the Allendale Rural Arts Team & runs an after-school program for local kids whose parents commute two hours & back to work at Hilton Head. But the census doesn't lie. Two kinds of folks leave town: those who can afford to & those who die.

/ not
incorporeal but materiality in motion, turning from one dimension & returning to another / not indexical of the conditions of social life but of the interiority only it engenders. In the museum in the notebook I stand in front of *Rail*, one of his black paintings. Fifteen

feet of topographical impasto, of etymological map: *rail* as noun, *rail* as verb, raiment & complaining, structural support & a wound flowing. Through these meanings he drives a thick black bar the shape of a tie, sticky & weeping creosote like this stack beside the tracks in Ulmer, South Carolina.

From the interior I drive southeast through Lowcountry palmettos, pine & live oak, a long smooth descent across coastal plain to the sea islands. After his breakup with R, Johns makes anguished gray canvases with titles like *Liar* & *Fool's House*. He reads the poems of Hart Crane, whose suicide he obliquely alludes to in *Periscope* & *Diver*, & leaves Manhattan for a beach house on Edisto Island, a purchase, he says, that changes his life

time passes

lines change

"Hot & humid, there was the smell
of warm breezes," John Giorno writes of Edisto. Johns' lover in 1968, he remembers "Jasper was happy because he felt at home in the South. He loved it." His house sits on the island's southern arc, which hosts a resort now. The rest is farm, marsh, Gullah Geechee property squeezed by developers & park on former plantations. At Botany Bay on the island's protected northeast edge I walk hushed & slow in full sun past Bleak Hall's low brick ruins, through fields of sunflower & corn the state maintains to feed wildlife. I walk due east, high tide coming in fast

lines continue

colors change

over the raised dirt path to the hammock island beyond salt marsh. I wade through warm water to a strip of dry land that lips the Atlantic. Ghost forest extends twenty feet out, a tangle of deadfall & upright trunks. In a bleached tree a black vulture preens, fabulous shadow the sea keeps. Nation's edge – Cusabo land, plantation land, Gullah Geechee land, wetland – it gives way to ocean rise. Nothing so flagless as this piracy.

FLAG, 1960

Sculp-metal & collage on canvas with Sculp-metal on wood frame
13⅛ x 11 ¼ inches

a stranger   a watchman   i pass through   my looking looks back   over this flag for R

a gift johns promises ca. 1957   & only delivers   the year before they break up   gray

not just as a color   that avoids a color situation   gray as idea   condition   material

gray as an attachment broken   at the point of most intimate contact   so the mind hides it

from itself   to preserve it   in a fiction   that avoids the emotional   dramatic qualities

of saying goodbye   the gray johns says is a literal quality   unmoved & unmovable

here has the force   of a passion that causes pain   denied & stifled   a self that can't be

revealed or spoken of   R keeps it until his death   *unfrightened of the affection*

beginning with structure   the division of the whole into parts   the painting of a flag

john cage writes   has its precedent in the sonnet   the grand division of fourteen lines

into eight & six   cage doesn't suggest   this makes johns a poet   & this flag a love poem

the kind only johns can write   to glimpse what joys or pains   our eyes can share

or answer   to quote hart crane   a deflection   the way i too here throw my voice

still unable to give R   the one unbetrayable reply   whose accent no farewell can know

Not long ago in our flat I pack for South Carolina, a scene I see now as rehearsal. I can't understand why I'm crying. Each folded shirt feels worse. This elegiac suitcase. Once I start I don't stop again in the middle of this room of gray paintings. Kitchen things hang on canvases labeled like cardboard boxes packed to move out fast

                              the medium
                 has a limited range

                 the steps seem
                 to be well defined

                 accomplished by
                 discrete operations

his early paintings
revel in meaning's plasticity, exploiting the gap between the look of the object & the viewer's response to it. Targets, flags, maps, & numbers / a language game. But in interviews, Johns resists & resents being misrepresented or misread. I think of this as the paranoia of the poorly loved. A dogged, defensive posture Agnes shares. Even their preference for theme & variation seems fueled by anxious relation to love's inevitable loss

                                   first impulse
                          give the object

                          a position / place
                          the object (it had

                          a position to begin
                          with) next / change

                          the object's position
                          hope

the energy organizing these fragments

The bourgeoisie call & offer me a job. To have to leave to get the
help I need, to have to give up home for health insurance: during
the days we discuss it, the city grows more beautiful, the way
anything does when you know you're about to lose it. We keep
walking upward to talk as though on a hilltop we could gain a
vantage over circumstance, the city a cascade of facades incised by
the camera-lens clarity of California light

                                          fragments
                                          that seem attached
                                          to an environment

                                          A way of behaving

my friend Rick texts a photo of Johns
in old age leaning in close to R's 1955 combine *Interview*, a piece he
makes not long after they fall in love. Oil, fabric, found painting,
photographs, found drawing, lace, wood, envelope, found letter,
printed reproductions, toweling & newspaper on wood structure
with brick, string, fork, softball, nail, metal hinges & wood door
is what it feels like inside my body, an affective state 72 ¾ × 49 ¼ ×
25 inches. It's the precise size of when there are no words

            To begin to do

A certain kind
of behavior but
also a certain
kind of attitude   (which might or
                          might not include
A new responsibility   a way to end
A new function
A new description

Agnes says *Stand with your back to the turmoil*. For years I think I can get it right. But there's no right way to be ill. No one can show the way through care broken in general & also broken in ways specific to my life. & no one can tell me how to be ill & how to pay for it, how to work, love & write at the same time. So I stand to face the turmoil: contest the bill, ask for the sliding scale, argue the diagnosis, insist on better listening. I take notes; I take the bourgeois job. Then I what.

I have an idea for a picture

just a detail I want to use

the painting isn't formed

but there's enough to be done

that I can start doing it

a painting called *Studio*
over twelve feet long & seven feet high. It looks like a mind that has space & time. It has a slanted door through which I want to bring R & a string of nine cans that ends in a brush hanging like a hooked fish. It has a star in long rays like a Defeo whose light I also want to share. Writing's how I might bring R through that door, how I might share with him the mind's made light. At his command I've cut the poem full of holes through which he falls away. In what appears to be home we are each alone. How to hold on to who we think we are? Rubber stamps & ink. Graphite marks. A ruler.

In the audience of a lecture I hear the critic say a poem's closure is a face turning away. I want to write the poem that closes by turning toward, going deeper into intimacy as it seems to end. I'm not Agnes, who jokes she feels happiest about a painting when it leaves her studio. In New Mexico she paints multiple versions of each vision she receives, variants so subtle others just see beauty. She asks her dealer to help her pick the best canvas & slice up the rejects with a knife. I'm still here a decade later, matching fragments to mend the present tense

I enclose a copy of a picture of us

Tawney writes to Agnes

walking into oblivion together

a spoon attached to a magnet
which can pivot on a hinge. A ruler attached with nails The letters of the word "NO" made of lead & suspended from a wire attached to the canvas with a screw eye. Split between his Edisto & Front St. studios, Johns makes objects to hold his abject status after he & R break up. I love the rueful single spoon of his new bachelorhood. The way it hangs small & almost camouflaged against lead-colored canvas / I love his *NO*, a negation made of a metal that's soft, easily damaged or lost – & toxic.

collage is fabric

depth is variable

Her hands are thinking

                    I have to choose. But I don't feel
free to lose anything else. I look at photos of Tawney at work. So
intimate with her warp, Indira Allegra notes, so explicit about her
relationship to her materials. Her touch opens negative space in the
woven form

      a gap for desire

                    to learn everything
abstract arises out of the material: the capacity to enjoy ideas, even
with destruction in them, & the bodily excitement that belongs to
them / a process that unfolds on the surface

                            to correct]what is faulty
                            to emend]a text
                            to recover]from illness
                            to repair   ]something broken
                            to heal   ]a person
                            to cure   ]a wound

to mend]its edges / to say her work is breath
she ties more than thirteen hundred separate ten-foot threads to a
canvas base she hangs from the ceiling. To each thread she gives
something of herself. To some she's movement through light & air.
To others, she's hidden in a cloud

                     & love just a knot, briefly, in
the visual field. I know it's time to choose. Here in the notebook I
make a net to catch

            when I fall into color forever

to bind the breath
that falls / to the one that rises

I love to watch the made thing take shape, *studio* & *study* the same root, *studium* a mode of enthusiasm, the line on the page like the hand-drawn line on gessoed canvas. Agnes uses a ruler & blue tape. Johns dips a very short brush into a saucepan of wax on a hot plate. After his breakup with R, he makes a painting to bite it. To say *Hello, object. I destroyed you. I love you.* After R & I break up, I can't make anything – the notebook

The possibility

of fineness
of broadness

empty / on the study floor I sit
unwilling to pack, to unmake the self I am with R, the self always being remade by illness, the self Agnes abjures as ego. "The error is in thinking," she says, "we have a part to play in the process." The sentence I make, the sentence I erase, the self that appears in phrases that vanish, wave-like, rushing forward to get nowhere really

what emerges in the one case
 " disappears "   " other "

Painting Bitten by a Man

is small – only 9 ½ x 7 inches – with a sticky pallor, the encaustic mucosal – the bite an injury he surely intends for R. It must fill his mouth with wax. "I want images to free themselves from me," Johns says. Perhaps another way to say *While I am loving you I am all the time destroying you.* What use is the object that doesn't survive love?

to twist	to rotate
to bend	to fire
to roll	to curve

to make a life together
like Richard Serra's *Doubled Torqued Ellipse*, two nested curved steel
walls twelve feet tall. They lean into & toward each other without
touching. When I enter it, I'm aroused by the act. At first it feels
weird to get hard in here. Then I think *This is Daddy's big slit*, his
warm hard inner walls pulsing in vertical runs of rust, subject &
object folding into each other as I walk. It looks like masculine
intimacy sometimes feels, emotionally distant & intense, unyielding
& enclosing

to dig	to stretch
to knot	to tighten
to flow	to gather

the center's
clear ring into which light & shadow fall shaped by the aperture
above. I watch the way the walls register chemical change in
gradients, delicate variants of fox & ferrous, the way R blushes
when he comes. I didn't mean to write that – I meant to fuck it.
When we break up it releases a flood of love so tall & broad I stand
for weeks inside it, the feeling sent back out into the world when
you let a beloved object go

to expand	of time
to surfeit	to continue
to light	

We live past the end of love & don't know it, despite intense sensation, a circle or an oval, a sort of spectrum twist. We say one thing is not another thing. Love ends the way health ends, in a copy that resembles the original, but whose materials have been shifted, a newspaper made of lead ⟵⟶ a metal paper bag

> one thing made
> of another
>
> one thing used
> as another

I don't understand / I think I'm trying / I can't
remember. When the nurse practitioner says "cognitive fog," it sounds pleasant, like marine layer hovering over the city most mornings. Distinguishing one thing from another ⟶ side by side, one on top of the other, one inside the other, one around the other. The essence of an object has some relation with its destruction. Turns out it's an imitation of the shape of my body. I'm trying, I think. All the objects slam shut, withdrawn into themselves

>] none has existed
>] none has been said to exist
>] none has been made

we say
we make love but we say a lot less about how we unmake it. The thickness of the paint. The kind of paint. The drying time (as though thought were rapid) & flesh color shadow. Only when I go to hold his hand & R pulls it away do I understand, suddenly & completely: I will lose everything when I leave & I will never get it back.

A mosaic of quotation, I lie down on the healer's table. I bring her my compendium of identifications: this body, the dearth of the author. My headache gripped in her hands, I feel the grid, how to stand at its edge & look out is to turn toward emptiness without form. When her palms gently flex against my occiput, a painless liquid silver fills my skull –

> Odd that any thing is arrived
> at, if it is

                                        what's the word
for this unanticipated gift? What's the word for this queer technology of association, this intimate contact site charged with sensuality? The poem! It floods with unfettered gratitude for everyone, every book, all the art I've ever loved, the sweet weave of what remains of me each time I fall into loss. It's why I need the grid, its tension

                              To describe the space
                              "   "   the system

                              in relation to everything
                              that is given

necessary to catch
& hold the self in all its constituent & contesting parts. Thank you Agnes. Thank you Johns. Thank you Ruth, Kathleen, Barbara & Wanda, Thom, Lauren, Eva, Lenore, Jay, Kiki & Sam. Thank you R, Miranda, Rick, Antje, Marintha & on & on in the bibliographic dark. In all the years I'm ill, am I ever able to offer adequate care to others, my beloveds? If to heal is to make meaning without injury to myself or others –

                      has it started yet? I hear: my mother
say *You better not lose your friend*, the distant distraught man weep in the hospital, the rough voice of the nurse say hello, the EMT strap me onto the gurney. What's that even mean

                              I ask the emergency again.

This is the artless part

                       my quietness has a man in it, a number of
naked selves, all the objects that fall from a life lived together taken
apart. Our blue bedroom has the look of a museum, each thing
alienated from its use until against my will / against my love they
all become art. Each sentence a lit vitrine, each paragraph a wall
text, even the one source of illumination disarticulated, cast in
plaster: bulb, socket, wire

                     <u>an arrogant object</u>

                            something to be folded or bent
                            or stretched.

                            SKIN

/ what we cannot speak
about," writes Ludwig, "we must pass over in silence." So here is
quietness in which the genius of things is speech, domestic
confessions I change into history: the spooning spoons tied
together, the cup on its hook, the tea towel folded neatly away.
This string of tin cans. Half a chair for half a man. The door with
no knob for him to grip. & here hangs the worn corn broom with
which I will sweep this fool's house clean.

Will there be a straight line at the beginning. Yes. Will there be a straight line at the end. Yes. "Horizontal lines for forty years," Agnes says, "Must be some kind of record." She knows beforehand how a painting will look: she has a vision, & the difficulty lies in reproducing it at scale, first at 6 x 6 & then, when she's in her 80s & no longer able to turn a 6 x 6 canvas, at 5 x 5. Here she stands in front of a table upon which is spread a large page of cramped calculations. "It doesn't look very hard but it is," she says, "How wide four blue bands would be." I'm surprised Johns ever allows some of his sketchbook pages to be reproduced & transcribed – even their workmanly concerns seem to reveal too much. "One would like not to be led," he writes. Later, in the documentary, he says: "Often in my choices I go through a kind of process of psychological disturbance . . . but that allows for a complexity in one way or another." For five years I think all I want is not to feel physical pain. I don't know what love has to do with it. I don't know what writing has to do with it. I don't know what painting has to do with it. Now I think I want less than something & more than nothing: the weight of *ink* on paper, of handwriting on the eye, its constancy this comfort or symptom in pencil –

In the notebook I linger, reluctant to leave. Since the emergency, wordlessness stays close, cold element that scours my mind lobe by lobe, frontal, occipital, parietal, temporal –

                          & remember the sudden
comfort of my own knowing returning: in the ear against the hospital pillow my heartbeat scratches like a field mouse settling back into its nest. I hear in the move from pictorial image to hidden subject the murmur of interpretation, all the hurt colors competing where feelings retreat & leave objects behind

                                 canvases
somatic as bodywork

                           the healer Marintha
cups my occiput again & pulls up gently. The migraine goes all aurora, hot pour of green closer to yellow in folds. Author of colors without words, she fingers the shut plates of my skull until they relent, release a clear gleam

                    the touch of consciousness upon itself

the knowledge of being here / in-folded

                         asleep in her thinking
hands / what it means to me

                  though Johns eschews interpretation
– "I don't think you can talk about art & get anywhere" – & Agnes insists on her own – "These paintings are about freedom from this world" – I believe care's the core of interpretative work, fragment of an immense form of mending together.

                             a painting can't wake up

                             from wordlessness & say

this roseate stain
on the last page

this skewed blue
crossed by contrails

what is color
but a kind of bliss

the leafcutter lifts
its green shape

across social space
the shade of maples

dark as this type
you draw near

to search the face
that won't turn away

[2007 – 2022]

QUOTING IS BITING

& it is also, as Katherine McKittrick argues in *Dear Science & Other Stories*, "a story, one of many, about how we know, how we come to know, & how we share what we know." This poem is a book-length collage whose primary sources are my own journals, notebooks & published & unpublished poems from 2007 to the present. It also borrows extensively from Jasper Johns' *Writings, Sketchbook Notes, Interviews* as well as from Agnes Martin's *Writings*. Some of their material is attributed & some unattributed, but I'd like to acknowledge that much fragmentary material embedded in the verse paragraphs comes from Johns' sketchbooks. In the brief sections about other artists & poets – Ruth Asawa, Kathleen Fraser, Thom Gunn, Kiki Smith, Jay Defeo, Eva Hesse, Lenore Tawney, Sam Gilliam & Richard Serra – I use oral histories, documentaries, artist's writings, art criticism, biographies & my own personal, museum & archival experiences as sources. In keeping with the gestural & intertextual nature of my notebook practice, small borrowings – lines & phrases – from other sources often go unmarked &/or unattributed. The following bibliography contains all secondary source texts – with gratitude to the authors & artists – as well as reference materials that offered information, correctives, inspiration & companionship in the archives of abstraction.

Anderson, Laurie. *Heart of a Dog.* Nonesuch Records, 2015.

Ashbery, John. *Reported Sightings: Art Chronicles 1957–1987.* Edited by David Bergman. Harvard University Press, 1989.

_____. *Selected Prose.* Edited by Eugene Richie. University of Michigan Press, 2004.

_____. *Something Close to Music: Late Art Writings, Poems, Playlists.* Edited by Jeffrey Lependorf. David Zwirner Books, 2022.

Barthes, Roland. *The Responsibility of Forms: Critical Essays on Music, Art, & Representation.* Translated by Richard Howard. University of California Press, 1991.

Batchelor, David. *Chromophobia.* Reaktion Books, 2000.

Baudelaire, Charles. *Selected Writings on Art & Artists.* Translated by P. E. Charvet. Penguin Books, 1972.

Benjamin, Walter. *The Writer of Modern Life: Essays on Charles Baudelaire*. Harvard University Press, 2006.

Berlant, Lauren. *On the Inconvenience of Other People*. Duke University Press, 2022.

____. *The Queen of America Goes to Washington City: Essays on Sex & Citizenship*. Duke University Press, 1997.

Bernstein, Roberta. *Jasper Johns: Catalogue Raisonné of Painting & Sculpture*. The Wildenstein Plattner Institute & Yale University Press, 2016.

Binstock, Jonathan P. *Sam Gilliam: A Retrospective*. University of California Press, 2005.

Blackwood, Michael, dir. *Jasper Johns: Decoy*. Michael Blackwood Productions, 1972.

Blocker, Jane. *What the Body Cost: Desire, History & Performance*. University of Minnesota Press, 2004.

Borden, Lizzie. Letter to Suzanne Delehanty. Undated. TS. University of Pennsylvania Rare Books & Manuscripts Library, Philadelphia.

Burgard, Timothy Anglin & Daniell Cornell, eds. *The Sculpture of Ruth Asawa: Contours in the Air*. University of California Press, 2020.

Cage, John. *A Year from Monday: New Lectures & Writings*. Wesleyan University Press, 1969.

Cavell, Stanley. *In Quest of the Ordinary: Lines of Skepticism & Romanticism*. University of Chicago Press, 1988.

Chadwick, Whitney & Isabelle de Courtivron, eds. *Significant Others: Creativity & Intimate Partnership*. Thames & Hudson, 1993.

Chase, Marilyn. *Everything She Touched: The Life of Ruth Asawa*. Chronicle Books, 2020.

Clare, Eli. *Brilliant Imperfection: Grappling with Cure*. Duke University Press, 2017.

Cooke, Lynne & Karen Kelly, eds. *Richard Serra: Torqued Ellipses*. Dia Art Foundation, 2015.

Cowie, Jefferson. *Freedom's Dominion: A Saga of White Resistance to Federal Power*. Basic Books, 2022.

Crane, Hart. *The Complete Poems*. Edited by Brom Weber. The Franklin Library, 1979.

Crase, Douglas. *The Revisionist & The Astropastorals*. Nightboat Books, 2019.

Crichton, Michael. *Jasper Johns*. Whitney Museum of Art & Harry N. Abrams, 1977.

Davidson, Michael. *Guys Like Us: Citing Masculinity in Cold War Poetics*. University of Chicago Press, 2003.

de Antonio, Emile, dir. *Painters Painting*. New Yorker Films, 1973.

de Certeau, Michel. *The Practice of Everyday Life*. Translated by Stephen Rendall. University of California Press, 1984.

DeFeo, Jay. *Works on Paper*. Edited by Bart Schneider. Kelly's Cove Press, 2015.

Deleuze, Gilles & Felix Guattari. *Kafka: Toward a Minor Literature*. Translated by Dana Polan. University of Minnesota Press, 1986.

DinéYazhí, Demian. *my ancestors will not let me forget this.* 2019. Glass, neon, aluminum frame, 42 × 22 × 23 in.

Eliot, T. S. *Collected Poems: 1909–1962.* Harcourt, Brace, & World, 1963.

Elliott, Chiyuma. *At Most.* Unicorn Press, 2020.

_____. *Blue in Green.* University of Chicago Press, 2021.

Engberg, Siri, ed. *Kiki Smith: A Gathering, 1980–2005.* Walker Art Center, 2005.

Epstein, Andrew. *Beautiful Enemies: Friendship & Postwar American Poetry.* Oxford University Press, 2006.

Eribon, Didier. *Insult & the Making of the Gay Self.* Translated by Michael Lucey. Duke University Press, 2004.

_____. *Returning to Reims.* Translated by Michael Lucey. Semiotext(e), 2013.

Ferenczi, Sándor. "Confusion of Tongues Between the Adult & the Child." In *Thalassa,* translated by Michael Balint, 225-30. The Psycho-Analytic Quarterly Inc, 1938.

Finney, Nicky. *Rice.* TriQuarterly, an imprint of Northwestern University Press, 2013.

Fleischmann, T. *Time Is the Thing A Body Moves Through.* Coffee House Press, 2019.

Foucault, Michel. *Discipline & Punish: The Birth of the Prison.* Translated by Alan Sheridan. Vintage Books, 1995.

Fraser, Kathleen. *Each Next: Narratives.* The Figures, 1980.

Gabriel, Mary. *Ninth Street Women: Lee Krasner, Elaine de Kooning, Grace Hartigan, Joan Mitchell, & Helen Frankenthaler: Five Painters & the Movement That Changed Modern Art.* Little Brown, 2018.

Gass, William. "Johns." *New York Review of Books,* February 2, 1989.

Gervitz, Gloria. *Migrations: Poem, 1976   2020.* Translated by Mark Schafer. New York Review of Books, 2020.

Getsy, David J., ed. *Queer.* Whitechapel Gallery & MIT Press, 2016.

_____. "Ten Queer Theses on Abstraction." In *Queer Abstraction,* edited by Jared Ledesma, 65–75. Des Moines Art Center, 2019.

Gilliam, Sam. "Oral history interview with Sam Gilliam, 1989 Nov. 4–11." By Benjamin Forgey. Smithsonian Archives of American Art. https://sova.si.edu/record/AAA.gillia89?t=C&q=*%3A*&i=0

Giorno, John. *Great Demon Kings: A Memoir of Poetry, Sex, Art, Death, & Enlightenment.* Farrar, Straus, & Giroux, 2020.

Glimcher, Arne. *Agnes Martin: Paintings, Writings, Remembrances.* Phaidon Press, 2012.

_____. *Sam Gilliam: Existed Existing.* Pace Gallery, 2020.

Goodman, Paul. "Advance-Guard Writing, 1900–1950." *The Kenyon Review* 13 no. 3 (Summer 1951): 357–380.

Green, Jane & Leah Levy, eds. *Jay DeFeo & The Rose.* University of California Press & Whitney Museum of Art, 2003.

Guest, Barbara. *Poems: The Location of Things, Archaics, The Open Skies*. Doubleday & Company, 1962.

Gunn, Thom. September–November 1968 notebook, Thom Gunn Papers, Bancroft Library, University of California-Berkeley.

_____. September 28, 1981–October 1983 notebook, Thom Gunn Papers, Bancroft Library, University of California-Berkeley.

_____. May 23, 1994–January 30, 1997 notebook, Thom Gunn Papers, Bancroft Library, University of California-Berkeley.

Hammons, David. *Body Prints: 1968–1979*. The Drawing Center, 2021.

Hejinian, Lyn. *My Life*. Sun & Moon Press, 1987.

Hesse, Eva. *Diaries*. Edited by Barry Rosen & Tamara Bloomberg. Hauser & Wirth Publishers, 2016.

Hopkins, Gerard Manley. *Poems*. Edited by Robert Bridges. Oxford University Press, 1933.

Hudson, Suzanne. *Agnes Martin: Night Sea*. Afterall Books, 2016.

Johns, Jasper. *Jasper Johns: Writings, Sketchbook Notes, Interviews*. Edited by Kirk Varnedoe. Museum of Modern Art, 1996.

Johnston, Jill. *Gullibles Travels*. Links Books, 1974.

_____. *Jasper Johns: Privileged Information*. Thames & Hudson, 1996.

Kafer, Alison. "After Crip, Crip Afters." *The South Atlantic Quarterly* 120, no. 2 (April 2021): 415–434.

_____. *Feminist Queer Crip*. Indiana University Press, 2013.

Kafka, Franz. "Advocates." *The Complete Stories*. Edited by Nahum N. Glatzer, 449-51. Schocken Books, 1971.

Katz, Jonathan D. "Agnes Martin & the Sexuality of Abstraction." In *Agnes Martin*, edited by Lynne Cooke & Karen Kelley, 171-97. Dia Foundation & Yale University Press, 2011.

Kyger, Joanne. *All This Every Day*. Big Sky, 1975.

_____. *Some Life*. The Post-Apollo Press, 2000.

Lancaster, Lex Morgan. *Dragging Away: Queer Abstraction in Contemporary Art*. Duke University Press, 2022.

Lance, Mary, dir. *Agnes Martin: With My Back to the World*. New Deal Films, 2003.

Lauterbach, Ann. *The Night Sky: Writings on the Poetics of Experience*. Penguin Books, 2005.

Léger, Nathalie. *Suite for Barbara Loden*. Translated by Natasha Lehrer & Cécile Menon. Dorothy, a Publishing Project, 2016.

Lemon, Ralph. "In My Mother's Voice." *Jasper Johns: Mind/Mirror*. Edited by Carlos Basualdo & Scott Rothkopf, 141-43. Philadelphia Museum of Art, Whitney Museum of American Art, & Yale University Press, 2021.

Leonard, Zoe. "A Wild Patience." *Agnes Martin.* Edited by Lynne Cooke & Karen Kelley, 80-101. Dia Foundation & Yale University Press, 2011.

Lessing, Gotthold Ephraim. *Laocoön: An Essay on the Limits of Painting & Poetry.* Translated by Edward Allen McCormick. The Bobbs-Merrill Company, 1962.

Lippincott, Robin. *Blue Territory: A Meditation on the Life & Art of Joan Mitchell.* Tidal Press, 2015.

Loden, Barbara, dir. *Wanda.* Foundation for Filmmakers, 1970.

Mangan, Kathleen Nugent, ed. *Lenore Tawney: A Retrospective.* American Craft Museum & Rizzoli, 1990.

Marlatt, Daphne. *Readings from the Labyrinth.* NeWest Press, 1998.

Martin, Agnes. *Writings.* Ed. Dieter Schwarz. Hantje Cantz, 2005.

Matory, J. Lorand. *Stigma & Culture: Last-Place Anxiety in Black America.* University of Chicago Press, 2015.

McCormick, Seth. "'In Memory of My Feelings': Jasper Johns, Pscyhoanalysis, & the Expressive Gesture." *Notes in the History of Art* 27 no. 2/3 (Winter/Spring 2008): 82–89.

McKittrick, Katherine. *Dear Science & Other Stories.* Duke University Press, 2021.

Menand, Louis. *The Free World: Art & Thought in the Cold War.* Farrar, Straus, & Giroux, 2021.

Miller, Dana. *Jay DeFeo: A Retrospective.* Whitney Museum of American Art, 2012.

Miller, Wes, dir. Ruth Asawa: *Of Forms & Growth. Masters & Masterworks Productions,* 1978.

Motika, Stephen. *Private Archive.* Albion Books, 2016.

_____. *Western Practice* Alice James Books, 2012.

Mulry, Megan & Chelsea Weathers, eds. *Agnes Martin: Independence of Mind.* Radius Books, 2022.

Myles, Eileen. *Chelsea Girls.* Black Sparrow Press, 1994.

_____. *Inferno (A Poet's Novel).* OR Books, 2010.

Nelson, Maggie. *The Argonauts.* Graywolf Press, 2015.

_____. *Bluets.* Wave Books, 2009.

_____. *Women, the New York School, & Other True Abstractions.* University of Iowa Press: 2007.

Notley, Alice. *Mysteries of Small Houses.* Penguin Books, 1998.

O'Hara, Frank. *Art Chronicles 1954–1966.* George Braziller, 1975.

_____. "In Memory of My Feelings." *Collected Poems.* Edited by Donald Allen, 252-57. University of California Press, 1995.

Orton, Fred. *Figuring Jasper Johns.* Harvard University Press, 1994.

Patterson, Karen E., ed. *Lenore Tawney: Mirror of the Universe.* John Michael Kohler Arts Center & University of Chicago Press, 2019.

Phillips, Adam. *Missing Out: In Praise of the Unlived Life.* Farrar, Straus, & Giroux, 2012.

Princenthal, Nancy. *Agnes Martin: Her Life & Art.* Thames & Hudson, 2015.

Raganelli, Katja, dir. *I Am Wanda: Barbara Loden.* Diorama Film, 1991.

Rivera Garza, Christina. *The Restless Dead: Necrowriting & Disappropriation.* Translated by Robin Myers. Vanderbilt University Press, 2020.

Rogers, Anna Backman. *Still Life: Notes on Barbara Loden's* Wanda *(1970).* Punctum Books, 2021.

Ronk, Martha. *In a landscape of having to repeat.* Omnidawn Publishing, 2004.

Roth, Moira. "The Aesthetics of Indifference." *Art Forum* 16 no. 3, (November 1977): 46-53.

Searson, Louis Arthur. *The Town of Allendale: A Gem of the South Carolina Low Country.* Columbia, 1949.

Sedgwick, Eve Kosofsky. *Touching Feeling: Affect, Pedagogy, & Performativity.* Duke University Press, 2003.

Schelling, Andrew. *Wild Form & Savage Grammar: Poetry, Ecology, Asia.* La Alameda Press, 2003.

Schlosberg, Jon, Briana Stewart, & Linsey Davis. "Residents of Allendale, SC's 'forgotten' county say 'Black voters need to be heard. They need to be recognized.'" *ABC News.* February 29, 2020. abcnews.go.com/Politics/residents-allendale-scs-forgotten-county-black-voters-heard/story?id=69266929

Serra, Richard. *Writings/Interviews.* University of Chicago Press, 1994.

Sharpe, Christina. *In the Wake: On Blackness & Being.* Duke University Press, 2016.

Sherry, Michael S. *Gay Artists in Modern American Culture: An Imagined Conspiracy.* University of North Carolina Press, 2007.

Silver, Kenneth E. "Modes of Disclosure: The Construction of Gay Identity & the Rise of Pop Art." In *Hand-Painted Pop: American Art in Transition, 1955–62,* edited Russell Ferguson, 179-203. Museum of Contemporary Art & Rizzoli International Publications, 1992.

Sloan, Aisha Sabatini. *Dreaming of Ramadi in Detroit. 1913* Press, 2017.

Snediker, Michael. *Contingent Figure: Chronic Pain & Queer Embodiment.* University of Minnesota Press, 2021.

Snowden, Yates & Harry Gardner Cutler, eds. *The History of South Carolina.* The Lewis Publishing Company, 1920.

South Carolina Department of Natural Resources. "Botany Bay Plantation WMA Driving Tour." November 2, 2022. https://dc.statelibrary.sc.gov/handle/10827/46654

South Carolina Office of Rural Health. "Coronavirus Hero: Meet Lottie Lewis." June 20, 2020. scorh.net/2020/06/12/coronavirus-hero-meet-lottie-lewis/

Stein, Gertrude. *Tender Buttons*. Sun & Moon Press, 1991.

Steinberg, Leo. *Jasper Johns*. George Wittenborn, 1963.

Stevens, Wallace. *The Necessary Angel: Essays on Reality & the Imagination*. Vintage Books, 1951.

Stockton, Kathryn Bond. *Gender(s)*. MIT Press, 2021.

Sussman, Elisabeth. *Eva Hesse*. San Francisco Museum of Modern Art, 2002.

Teare, Brian. *[black sun crown]*. Fact-Simile Press, 2013.

_____. *The Empty Form Goes All the Way to Heaven*. Ahsahta Press, 2015.

Tejada-Flores, Rick, dir. *Jasper Johns: Ideas in Paint*. American Masters, 1989.

Theroux, Paul. *Deep South: Four Seasons on Back Roads*. Houghton Mifflin Harcourt, 2015.

Tomkins, Calvin. *Off the Wall: Robert Rauschenberg & the Art of Our Time*. Doubleday, 1980.

Truitt, Anne. *Yield: The Journal of an Artist*. Princeton University Press, 2022.

Turkle, Sherry. *Psychoanalytic Politics: Jacques Lacan & the French Revolution*. The Guilford Press, 1992.

Winnicott, D. W. "Fear of Breakdown." *International Review of Psychoanalysis* 1, no 1-2 (1974): 103–07.

_____. *Home Is Where We Start From: Essays by a Psychoanalyst*. W.W. Norton, 1990.

_____. *Playing & Reality*. Routledge, 2005.

Wittgenstein, Ludwig. *On Certainty*. Edited by G. E. M. Anscombe & G. H. von Wright. Harper & Row, 1972.

Woolf, Virginia. *Jacob's Room*. Harcourt Brace, 1960.

_____. "On Being Ill" *The Moment & Other Essays*. Edited by Leonard Woolf, 9-23. Harcourt Brace, 1975.

Wright, C.D. *String Light*. University of Georgia Press, 1991.

_____. *Jean Valentine, Abridged: "writing a word/changing it."* Albion Books, 2011.

GRATITUDE

: to the editors of *Kenyon Review, New England Review, Massachusetts Review* & *The Rumpus*, who published pages from this poem, sometimes in much earlier versions.

: to the Guggenheim Foundation & the University of Virginia, without whose support I would not have had the space and time to write this book.

: to the caregivers & healers Cynthia Allred-Jackson, Antje Hofmeister, Sam Pierceall, Dr. Meghna Shah, Amina Stevens, Marintha Tewksbury, Dr. Heidi Wittels & Eva Zeller, without whose care my life would not be possible.

: to Carlos Basualdo, Greg Stuart, Sarah B. Vogelman & Linnea West at the Philadelphia Museum of Art, whose generous commission instigated this book.

: to Kim Bears-Bailey, Patricia Lent & R. H. Quaytman for conversations about Johns, R, Cunningham & their legacy.

: to Rick Barot, Khadijah Queen & Cole Swensen for the time spent writing into & through Johns' body of work together.

: to Victoria Chang for conversations about Agnes & ekphrasis.

: to Jaime Shearn Coan for conversations about Agnes & for the concept of "critical ekphrasis."

: to Rick Barot & Gillian Conoley, peerless first readers.

: & to Stephen Motika for believing in & supporting this book during its composition, & to Lina Bergamini, Lindsey Boldt, Jaye Elizabeth Elijah, Gia Gonzales & Kit Schluter for making it real.

A 2020 Guggenheim Fellow, Brian Teare is the author of eight chapbooks and seven critically acclaimed books, including *Companion Grasses*, a finalist for the Kingsley Tufts Award, and *Doomstead Days*, winner of the Four Quartets Prize and a finalist for the National Book Critics Circle, Kingsley Tufts, and Lambda Literary Awards. His most recent publications are a pair of book-length ekphrastic projects exploring queer abstraction, chronic illness, and collage: the 2022 reissue of *The Empty Form Goes All the Way to Heaven*, and the 2023 publication of *Poem Bitten by a Man*. His honors include Lambda Literary and Publishing Triangle Awards, and fellowships from the NEA, the Pew Foundation, the American Antiquarian Society, the Headlands Center for the Arts, the Vermont Studio Center, and the MacDowell Colony. After over a decade of teaching and writing in the San Francisco Bay Area, and eight years in Philadelphia, he's now an Associate Professor of Poetry at the University of Virginia. An editorial board member of *Poetry Daily*, he lives in Charlottesville, where he makes books by hand for his micropress, Albion Books.

NIGHTBOAT BOOKS

Nightboat Books, a nonprofit organization, seeks to develop audiences for writers whose work resists convention and transcends boundaries. We publish books rich with poignancy, intelligence, and risk. Please visit nightboat.org to learn about our titles and how you can support our future publications.

The following individuals have supported the publication of this book. We thank them for their generosity and commitment to the mission of Nightboat Books:

Kazim Ali • Anonymous (8) • Mary Armantrout • Jean C. Ballantyne • Thomas Ballantyne • Bill Bruns • John Cappetta • V. Shannon Clyne • Ulla Dydo Charitable Fund • Photios Giovanis • Amanda Greenberger • Vandana Khanna • Isaac Klausner • Shari Leinwand • Anne Marie Macari • Elizabeth Madans • Martha Melvoin • Caren Motika • Elizabeth Motika • The Leslie Scalapino - O Books Fund • Robin Shanus • Thomas Shardlow • Rebecca Shea • Ira Silverberg • Benjamin Taylor • David Wall • Jerrie Whitfield & Richard Motika • Arden Wohl • Issam Zineh

This book is made possible, in part, by grants from the New York City Department of Cultural Affairs in partnership with the City Council, the New York State Council on the Arts Literature Program, and the National Endowment for the Arts.